LIFE IN ITS RAWEST FORM

LIFE IN ITS
RAWEST
FORM

A True Story of
Perseverance and Triumph

QIANA HICKS

Edited by Words That Flo! ... Editorial Consultancy Services
wordsrspirit@aol.com • (310) 619-9304

Edited by Mary Beth Ruhland • Editor and Publications Specialist • Eagan, MN
mbruhland@gmail.com • (651) 470-9519

Cover Design and Photograph by Derek Blanks Photography
Dblanks.com

Book design and production by Ryan Scheife/Mayfly Design
Mayflydesign.com

Visit the author website: www.qianahicks.com
Contact Information: wordsofinspirationpublishing@gmail.com

Words of Inspiration
PUBLISHING

Library of Congress Control Number: 2017903036
ISBN 978-0-9986180-0-5 (paperback), 978-0-9986180-1-2 (ePub),
978-0-9986180-2-9 (Kindle)

BIO023000 BIOGRAPHY & AUTOBIOGRAPHY/African American & Blacks
SEL021000 SELF-HELP/Motivational & Inspirational

DEDICATED TO...

I dedicate this book to those who took time to help me develop my story into something that has the potential to help others in similar circumstances. I expected to make this journey alone, with little support or guidance. The thought initially discouraged me. When I reached out to you, I felt confident and inspired to finish what I had started. Each of you reassured me as I made my way through my writing process, and I am forever grateful to you! Your passion to help others is what I needed to achieve this dream.

To my family, friends, and colleagues who didn't doubt my ability to write this book, thank you for believing in me and encouraging me. Your faith fueled my determination that I could do this, and anything else I set my mind to. You saw strength and potential I didn't know I had. I cherish our relationships, and look forward to strengthening them along the way.

ACKNOWLEDGMENTS

To my dear son, you have been mommy's champion from the moment this book was only a thought. You undoubtedly believed that I could do it and make something great of it. You are my *shining star*, the one person I can look to whenever I'm in doubt or feel discouraged. I am proud of the person you are becoming, and I love you more than words can express.

Dr. Thompson, thank you for taking time to read my story and provide feedback from a reader's point of view. Your opinions helped me flesh out ways that I could use my experiences to help others living in similar situations. I appreciate your support, and I graciously thank you.

Words That Flo!—Flo Jenkins, Natalie Rotunda, and Mary Beth, you took on my project with care, and you were a light in the dark as I began my journey into unfamiliar territory. You shared your experiences and your expertise to help my book evolve to where it is today. Thank you for your support and guidance. You are amazing people, editors, and writers. I am thankful for the opportunity to work with you.

To the most fabulous graphic designers, Ryan Scheife and Derek Blanks, thank for doing such an amazing job with my book. Your creativity and natural talent has allowed my book to capture the essence of my story *in its rawest form*. Thank you!

To my family, no matter what life throws our way, one fact never changes: we *will always be family*. We've endured a lot and have overcome it all. This should be a testament of how our love and closeness will always stand the test of time, because we were just built that way. Regardless of our ups and downs, we are all that we have. I love you. I hope our enduring love always keeps us close.

CONTENTS

PREFACE

For some of us, life is a breeze. For others, it is but a treacherous storm—like being born with "bad karma," where never-ending rough times and bad circumstances are their unfortunate reality. Hope or normalcy seems so farfetched from their world.

They question nearly everything, but mainly they ask why they were born and whether their birth was some sort of cruel and unusual punishment. Why can't their turmoil happen to others who are more deserving, they wonder. In their day-to-day existence, they may hopelessly question their faith. Is there a Higher Power—and, if so, why isn't this Power, this loving God, looking out for their best interests?

I know these wounded people, and I know their sad stories. I was one of them. I lived with their same questions and doubts, I was often discouraged from hoping for a better life. I certainly hadn't asked to be born into such harsh conditions, and I could not understand why I was *chosen* to endure them.

My purpose in writing this book to is to give youth going through similar circumstances hope and inspiration that will help them prevail through adversity. In addition to the youth, I pray that my book will give insight to young adults, Family Services professionals, therapists, educators, and others on how their help and support can make a positive difference in the lives of children and families facing oppression and troubled times. I also hope that it will enlighten parents on how their actions can negatively affect the lives of their loved ones.

I titled this book *Life In Its Rawest Form* because that's the life I was dealt; not only was it raw, it was *uncut, unpolished, and peeled to the core*. I don't claim this was either good or bad; it was just the hand I was dealt. How I played those cards is, perhaps, the more important story.

...Nothing came easy and everything was a struggle...

I used to think the saying, "Everything happens for a reason," was just a cliché and had no substance. I believe the saying now, because I've learned that life has its own "agenda," and that people aren't often given the option of dictating it. Life happens according to its own plan. My life's agenda of endless turmoil spanned 35-plus years.

Before I learned this lesson, I had wished to be the creator and manager of my own agenda and *choose* what happened and *choose* who had a part in it. As I grew wiser, I realized my agenda's Creator and Manager is much greater than I could ever have fathomed! My agenda was no different from others', but, somehow, it *made me different* from others I knew.

My life itself is a project that continues to evolve. I can't quite say that I am a finished product or deliverable, but I can say that I've been in production mode for quite some time, and it hasn't always been easy. I'm far from being in sustaining mode or having things all figured out, but the deliverance of each milestone just makes me even stronger for the one that comes next.

As a young girl, I felt compelled to write about events taking place in my life. I didn't understand why these things were happening to me. I had no one to confide in. Writing them down became a form of therapy, as I attempted to make sense of what was happening *to me* and *around me*. By writing things down, I was seeing things in a different light, in hopes of bringing clarity and closure.

Writing was also a silent sounding board. I could bounce theories and ideas around on paper to convince my young self that I was *not immoral* due to the impure events happening to me. Some events singled me out from other kids my age, making me feel I was ahead of my time.

When first thinking about writing my autobiography, I was reluctant. It would expose the dark times in my life. I was afraid of being judged or singled out more than I already had been. However, being able to console or help others living in circumstances similar to mine overshadowed my reluctance, fear, and anxiety. My intent in sharing my story isn't to hurt or defame anyone, but simply to provide relief to myself for the things I've harbored for years— while helping others at the same time. I hope that my words will reach those who feel *helpless* and *defeated* at times.

I'm hopeful that I can shed light on what I've learned: we don't get to totally choose what happens *to us* in life, but we can choose *whether we allow such circumstances to make or break us.*

Truly, life isn't easy, but if you put in the work, you can live a life as bright and shiny as the sun. It took me a while to move past the hurt and anger. If we allow ourselves to dwell on life's negatives, we create a life filled with darkness, with even bigger problems to come. Depression or thoughts of suicide can haunt or destroy us if we don't *fight* to overcome our past and to *accept those things we cannot change.*

The encouragement to improve one's life that you'll read within these pages, may seem easier said than done, but your life is what you make of it. It is my intent, my hope, that after you read this book, your outlook on life will be different and better. Remember, it's never too late to change. Let us accept our past as one of many things that makes us different and unique. It's not necessarily good or bad; *it is what it is.* If we—*you and I*—are fortunate enough to get through it, then we've been given another chance to make a difference in the world *by doing better.*

ONE

Where It All Began

was born in Gary, Indiana, the middle child of three. My mother was 19 when she had my brother, 21 when she had me, and 27 when she had my sister. My parents married when my mother was pregnant with my older brother. As to my biological father, I vaguely remember life with him. He left when I was a couple years old.

I do remember when I was 1½ years old, that both my mother and father lived under the same roof in a small duplex that sat much further back from the sidewalk than other houses on that block. My mother and family members said my father physically abused her during their time together.

The only memory I have of my father is of him spanking me for jumping in the bed after being told not to. In addition to being spanked, I had to stand in the corner, facing the wall in the living room. It's the last memory I have of my parents, my brother, and me living together as a complete family. Around that time, my father went to prison for being an accomplice in a bank robbery.

It seemed like a short time after my father went to prison that my mother met my sister's dad. I was two or three years old, and remember going with mommy to visit him at a mutual friend's house in one of Gary's many housing projects. Their relationship grew, and we became like a family. He naturally assumed the role and responsibilities of a father, and that's what my brother and I called him. From that point on, I'd always refer to him as my stepfather, even though they were never married.

In time, my mother's behavior and habits changed. I believe my stepfather introduced her to the lifestyle of alcoholism and drug abuse. At the time, I didn't know what type of drugs they were using, but I eventually recognized them by their smells and the items used to smoke them with. A price had to be paid for the substance abuse, and my brother and I were the ones who paid.

The relationship between my mother and "stepfather" was toxic. One minute they were happy together; the next, they were fighting and splitting up. Most arguments started while they were intoxicated. Arguments frequently grew into explosions that left my mother badly beaten. On several occasions, my brother and I witnessed my stepfather brutally beating our mother.

Each time, she was left with some physical damage. I saw him punch, kick, and manhandle her. He was a monster during those times. Once he got started, there was no stopping him. Sometimes, my mother's face was unrecognizable, it was so swollen and bruised. When my brother and I would try to defend her, we'd get pushed aside.

One of the nights we stayed over at my stepfather's house, I woke up in the middle of the night to them fighting. Again, he beat her, and, as always, she tried to fight back.

To escape from further beatings, my mother gathered my brother and me, and we walked several miles to our place on Delaware. We left with only the clothes on our backs, and my mom was barefoot. She walked fast, dragging my brother and me as she tried to help us keep up with her. It seemed no one else was walking the streets and alleys at that hour except us.

This love-hate relationship continued. When it got bad, it was bad.

Prior to my sister's birth, we mostly stayed at my stepfather's house on Ohio Street in Gary, where our living arrangements were good. He worked at the steel mill and my mother worked odd jobs here and there, but mostly she stayed home.

Even while living in his house, my mother had not let go of our place on Delaware, where we lived in the basement of a duplex and an elderly woman occupied the upstairs apartment. We had one small bedroom, a small sitting area, and a half bathroom; the bare minimum. The place was very dark and desolate, and extremely scary to me. I was four or five at the time. We were very poor. I have no happy memories of living there. In fact, I hated that house.

Aside from being extremely poor, my mother was sad and depressed when we stayed there. Friends whom she often visited and got high with lived on the corner near us. While visiting them, she would send my brother and me across the street to the corner apartment building, directly across from her friends' place.

From what I can remember, it was a large family who lived in that apartment building. The parents never seemed to be home, just the kids. We were forced to play outside with the kids while we were there. An older sibling watched over her siblings.

One day, the older sister called me into the house. I don't remember what for, but she must have said something to make me feel like it was okay. They lived in the downstairs apartment, similar to ours. I went in.

She told me to take off my clothes, and she ordered me to lie down. I was scared and confused. I was too afraid not to do what the girl wanted, or to fight back. She was big and intimidating. She did some uncomfortable things to me. I hated it. I was there alone with her, and I was terrified. I had never wanted my mother so badly. I wished that my brother and the other kids would come in and save me. After she was done, she sent me back outside to play. This went on a few times during our stay on Delaware.

I hated when my mother went to her friends' house and begged her not to send us across the street. But she didn't listen and I couldn't tell her the real reason why, because that monster of a girl made me keep it from everyone. Going to mom's friends' house was play for my brother, but hell for me. He had no idea what was going on and probably didn't even notice when I went missing for a while.

Eventually, we moved away from that place, and I never returned. I've managed to suppress those memories and to never think about them again. Until this day, I hadn't told anyone.

TWO

Coming of Age Too Soon

G rowing up in a disadvantaged or single-parent home can cause a person to mature faster than their years, forcing them into adult situations. Generally, the lack of parental guidance and supervision places an unreasonable amount of responsibility on children, particularly older siblings. They must often grow up and make adult-like decisions, depriving them of enjoying things for their own age group.

For some, functioning as a parent figure becomes not only a necessity, but also a natural responsibility. Often, they learn by trial and error, or from watching their parents. This pseudo-parenting role forces them into situations they may not be truly ready for, potentially putting them in harm's way. Long-term, children growing up in these circumstances may have developmental issues.

Psychological instability or identity crisis are possible outcomes for children who handle duties beyond their age. They may begin to actually think they *are* adults, and lose interest in the things and activities belonging to their own age group. The child often finds the company of older people more interesting than that of their peers. This can—and did, for me—lead to mistakes.

As early as six and four years old, respectively, my brother and I had to quickly learn the ropes of raising ourselves and staying afloat each day. By now, my mother's focus and priorities were my sister's father, drugs, and alcohol, which all led to countless motherless nights (even when she was *physically present* in our home). Every now and then, between coming down from a high and preparing for the next one, she managed to squeeze a little time in for my brother and me. We soaked up as much attention as we could, because those times didn't last long.

There were many days and nights when my brother and I were home alone, and we became accustomed to taking care of one another. The streets of Gary, Indiana, were treacherous, so we were often plagued by the ghosts of poverty, crime, and depression, especially at night.

My brother was my protector. As long as he was there with me, it was easier to bear the fear of being alone. We would take turns escorting one another to the bathroom, or wherever we had to go in the house. This helped to alleviate the fear of the unknown, and the fear of being in an empty house by ourselves.

We learned to take care of ourselves, such as bathe, get ourselves dressed, cook, and watch over one another while my mother was absent. The bond we formed made it difficult for me if my brother was away for any reason. He was the closest thing I had to a parent. Still, his protection and help didn't fill the empty void that only our mother and father would have filled. I'm sure my brother felt the same as I did, except he had a different way of dealing with it. For the most part, he suppressed his feelings and emotions, whereas I often whined and cried.

Six years into their relationship, my mother became pregnant, but she continued to use drugs. When my sister was born, I became to her what my brother was to me. My brother and I nurtured our infant sister, while our mother was out getting high or drunk every chance she got. This changed the dynamics for us, since it was now the three of us at home by ourselves, often with little to no food.

As an infant, my sister had frequent medical problems, like colic, and she would scream her lungs out, day and night, until she cried herself to sleep. My brother and I felt helpless. Most nights, we didn't have any baby milk for her, and we had nothing else to give her but water, which didn't help her most of the time. Nothing we did calmed or comforted her. It was painful to see her go through this. Many lonely nights, all we could do was close the door, turn off the lights, and let her cry herself to sleep.

As my sister grew older, I bonded with her as if I had given birth to her. She was my everything, and the two of us were everything to my brother. He provided protection to us on the nights we were left alone, while I provided the nurturing (cooking, cleaning, bathing my sister and combing her hair). He shared some of these responsibilities, too, but they fell mostly on me. We quickly established an operating rhythm and survived the best we knew how.

Often, we were left without food in the house; no baby food, or anything that came close to a full meal to satisfy our hunger. We learned to survive with water and bread. One would be amazed at how far sugar sandwiches, mayo sandwiches, and ketchup sandwiches could take you, and how handy newspaper and phone book pages were when there was no toilet tissue. Improvising was what we knew best.

Food wasn't the only thing we regularly lacked. On countless days and nights, we didn't have electricity and gas. Some nights, we literally had to pat our way through the dark to get to where we needed to go, relying on familiarity. When we had no electricity or water (due to nonpayment), we used snow to freeze or refrigerate what food we had.

On nights when we had no gas, we opened the oven door to keep warm. That didn't heat the rest of the house, so we stayed near the oven in the kitchen. When our water was shut off, we took empty two-liter soda pop bottles and milk jugs and filled them up in the neighbor's bathroom. It became so regular when we showed up at their door that they would direct us to the bathroom.

White rice was my least favorite food. One time, all we had was an open bag of rice. I had begged my mother to let my friends, Cindy and Emil, come over after church. She was reluctant, but finally gave into my relentless begging and pleading.

We were all hungry by the time we came home from church, so my mom fixed what was left of the rice—enough for each of us to have half a bowl. I ate every grain of rice and licked the butter and salt off the bowl when it was gone. My least favorite food became the best in the world that day, and I wanted more, but there wasn't any left.

I vividly remember the look on my mother's face as she watched me devour the rice and lick the bowl, as if it was my last meal. She had a look of sorrow in her eyes, along with a sad facial expression as she watched us eat. I knew that she wanted so badly to give me more. I could see the pain that filled her eyes as she looked on hopelessly, so I didn't bother to let her know I was really hungry for more. I didn't want her to hurt anymore from having to tell me there was nothing more to eat.

Throughout these hard times, my mother still left us alone to fend for ourselves. At times, I felt so hungry that I had fantasies of eating the food shown in the coupon section of the newspaper.

I vividly recall a summer day when my mom had been gone literally all day, and there was absolutely no food in the house. My brother and sister and I sat in the front room, watching out the window, hoping our mother would return with food.

Later that day, we went outside to play. I was lying on the concrete sidewalk, looking up at the sky. As I started to get up, I saw a car drive by—and my mom was in it. She tried to duck down so we wouldn't see her, but I saw her. I was certain it was her. An older white man we had never seen before was driving. I remember feeling devastated that she didn't stop. We had been waiting all day for her, starving and deprived, not only of food, but of her love and affection. I became angry and frustrated with her at that very moment. To make matters worse, she didn't come home until late that night. This became the norm for us.

My mother spent less and less time being a mother, and more and more time being a crack addict, alcoholic, and a girlfriend. It felt like we were at the bottom of her priority list. But not my sister. She was always at the top of my mother's list on the days she was sober and wanting to be a mother. It seemed like my sister was the only one my mother cared about of the three of us, perhaps because she was the youngest. But that didn't stop me from wishing she loved me the same way. I needed her just as much as my sister did, if not more. My sister had motherly love coming from both my mother and me, whereas I barely had any at all.

I longed for the love, affection, and attention that my mother gave my sister. I started to think that she cared more about my sister, because she cared so much for my sister's father at the time. It was like my brother and I mostly took the back seat, and that made me feel that she didn't need me at all.

I felt empty inside, because I could never get enough of her love. I craved my mother's love, and I needed her. She loved me, too, I knew, but I wanted the same hugs, kisses, and affection that she showered my sister with. I often wondered what it was like to be the center of mommy's world. Had she felt the same for me when I was my little sister's age?

For a time, we lived with my stepfather in a family-owned home on Kentucky Street, next to where his mother lived. She was nice to us and treated us like her biological grandkids. We referred to her as our grandmother.

The house we occupied had a flight of steep, wooden stairs. One day, I was trailing my mom down the stairs, holding my sister, while my mother was carrying a basket of laundry. I tripped on one of the garments hanging out of the basket, and went tumbling down, holding my sister tight. When we got to the bottom, my mother screamed hysterically for her baby. She grabbed my sister and comforted her.

It was as if I didn't exist. I was mortified, hurt, and crying. I was still shaken from the fall and the thought of my sister being hurt. Not once did my mother ask if I had been hurt, or check to see if I was okay. Instead, she fussed at me for falling with my sister, as if I could help it.

I was more hurt from her lack of compassion than from the bruises themselves. I felt like she could care less if I was seriously injured, as long as her baby was fine, and that scared me more than the fall.

Needless to say, things didn't get any better. The stronger my mother's addictions grew, the less of her love and attention trickled down to me. At one point, I bargained with my mom about her sobriety. When I learned she was going out, I would *beg* her not to get high or drunk, but she always did. She would tell me that she wouldn't, and that she was taking her "medicine" with her, just in case. Her medicine was cooking oil. She tried to convince me that it helped her stay sober and kept her from getting drunk. I was seven years old, so what did I know? I believed her and made sure she didn't forget her medicine.

When she came home, drunk and belligerent, she caused all kinds of chaos. She would find some reason to be upset and take it out on my brother and me, beating us until she either passed out or forgot what had made her upset.

As her alcohol addiction worsened, she became extremely hostile and violent toward my brother and me. Most of those times, my stepfather wasn't home. Had he been there, we most likely would have been safe, because he would have been abusing my mother, and getting abused by her.

My mother's drunken temperament kept me petrified of her going out, because I was afraid of getting beaten when she returned home. Some nights, we'd wake up to her beating us for no valid reason. I was so overcome with fear that I was afraid to eat; plus, I was afraid of vomiting the food already in my stomach. Being caught off guard and being beaten nauseated me—gave me butterflies in my stomach—it was just easier not to have a full belly during those times.

The nights seemed longer during these times, too, because I was too afraid to fall asleep. So, I fought sleep and stayed awake. I was in a no-win situation. Either way, it was torture. Morning couldn't come soon enough. I just wanted it all to be over.

Talking to my mother about it was useless. She'd just say it wouldn't happen again. But it always did.

My brother and I built defense mechanisms and tactics to defuse the craziness. We often did this by getting on her good side and talking nicely to her to keep her from going from 1 to 10 on the anger scale. Sometimes we succeeded, other times we didn't. When trouble happened, the best thing to do was to wish for the night to end sooner, or wish that she would fall asleep, whichever came first.

Like so many other kids in this predicament, we didn't have anyone to turn to. We were taught not to take our business outside of our home. If we did, we were usually in for some sort of cruel punishment. Knowing this, I was terrified to tell anyone or to ask for help for fear of getting a whipping or worse. I also felt a sense of loyalty or obligation to my mother not to tell anyone about what went on, even if it meant being neglected.

There was no one I could go to, anyway, even if I could have built up enough courage to ask for help. How we lived was no different from how a lot of people in our community lived. Those who didn't suffer like we did didn't do anything to help us, so my options for getting help were slim to none.

Had I known then what I know now, on nights when my mother went out, I would have asked if the three of us could spend the night at a neighbor's or a relative's house. That way, we wouldn't have been caught in the line of fire when she came home.

Another thing I would have done differently is talk to another adult, whether a parent of a friend, a neighbor, or someone at school. If we had had a phone back then, I probably would have dialed 911 when it started to get bad. Times are different now, because there are a lot more services that protect children from environments like the one we grew up in.

I would urge anyone living in these circumstances to reach out and tell someone. What we fail to realize, is that our parents need help, too. Speaking up would not only have put us in a safer setting, but it could have allowed my mother to get the help she needed, earlier on.

Key Takeaway from Chapter Two
Things I could have done differently.

- I would have talked to another adult—a parent of a friend, a neighbor, or someone at school, if conditions weren't improving at home.

- I would have called 911 when things got out of control and my siblings' lives and mine were in danger.

- I would have gotten help and not feared the consequences. Getting help may have benefited my parent(s), as well as my siblings and me.

- I would have lived within the moment by doing more age-appropriate activities, expanding on friendships in my age group, and enjoying my childhood and adolescence, instead of thinking and acting like an adult and taking on adult responsibilities.

- I would not have held myself responsible for the choices others made.

THREE

Things Are Forever Changing

Children forced to grow up in disadvantaged households benefit from familiar surroundings during times of unfortunate or unsafe conditions. While some children rely on neighbors or nearby relatives, others are not as fortunate. Nearby support gives relief and helps children feel confident that they have somewhere to turn when they need help.

Living with a parent or parents who battle substance abuse often places children in unsafe or harmful conditions, whether intentional or not. They're at greater risk, too, if constantly uprooted, because the support system they established for themselves is gone.

This instability can also later lead to major psychological issues, anxiety issues, and uncertainty, making settling down or long-term commitments more challenging than for those who lived a more stable life. Children may wonder about their place in life and how they can fit into society, because every time they get acclimated, something changes. Some are afraid to get comfortable or content in their surroundings, because change may come at any moment.

Instability can also lead to feeling *isolated*, because they don't know how to get used to things, or stability may seem abnormal. It became difficult for me, because we were constantly evicted, hopping from place to place, and shelter to shelter.

Planning for the future or seeing possibilities for a better, different life requires stability. Inconsistency may cause confusion, or create a lifestyle where a person only sees what's immediately in front of them; hence, making it difficult to plan for the future.

13

As children, we lost almost every home we had, because my mom didn't pay the rent. She managed to get money for her habits, but our bills and rent were often neglected. Having two addictions of the worst kind (drugs and alcohol) meant double the problems.

As my mother's and stepfather's habits grew stronger, keeping food in the refrigerator and our utilities paid became more difficult. There was no consistency in our lives, often keeping me guessing about what was next.

When I was seven years old, my mother sent us to Rochester, New York, to live with my great-aunt, while she stayed in Gary to straighten out her life and provide a better living for us. My sister remained with her. I didn't want to separate from my mom and my sister and begged her to let me stay, but she insisted it was best. She dropped us off at our grandmother's house where my great-aunt picked us up. As my mother left, I felt like it was the last time I would ever see her. I cried uncontrollably; it was so hard letting her go.

The feeling of missing my mother only grew stronger in Rochester. I longed to be in her arms. It didn't sit well with me that I couldn't be there to protect and care for my sister. I cried a lot at first, hoping I would see my mother and sister sooner rather than later.

Although my family took great care of my brother and me, it was nothing like having my mother's love, seeing her face and being close to her. I didn't care what her circumstances were; I just wanted to be with her again.

My great-aunt took care of us like we were her own children (she was doing the same for her grandkids at the time). I still missed my mother, but it felt good to have dedicated love. My great-aunt and grandmother spoiled me with love and affection, like they were overcompensating for my biological father, who, by the way, lived across the street from us with his mother.

We also spent a lot of time with my father's sister, who regularly came to get us to spend time with her and her family. She set an example of what it was like to live in a healthy, functioning family, and I enjoyed being with her, too. She was the ideal mother, wife, and spiritual leader. In fact, both of my father's sisters were. I wish some of what they had would have rubbed off on him.

My father spent the early part of my childhood in prison. After he was released, he still felt institutionalized, only this time by alcohol, not metal bars. He didn't try to make up for the time he'd lost being there for us. Instead, he became a perpetual drinker. The only difference between his addiction and my mother's, was that he didn't physically hurt us.

I used to wish that my father would take us away and be the All-American dad. Regardless of how absent he was from our lives, or how drunk he'd be when we visited him, I still wished for him to be in our lives. I used to fantasize about being a daddy's girl, and what it would feel like to see his smile every day when I woke up. I wanted so badly for him to be there for me and to be the positive male figure my brother needed as he was coming of age. Every time I called him "Daddy," I said it with so much joy, as if he was actually doing his part as a good father. It was my way of making my fantasy come true.

Sadly, the only real daddy in our lives was a spirit whom we could not see or physically hug; nor could we cry on His shoulder while He patted our backs and told us everything would be all right. However, we knew He was there and was looking out for us from the gates of heaven. God was the only true father we had.

My dad's dad did a pretty good job of picking up the slack for his son. Periodically, we spent nights with him when we lived in Gary. He bought us clothes, our first bikes, and he showed us what it was like to have a great father figure in our lives. I truly loved and cherished him; however, being with him only made me wish that he was my father.

My grandfather was a busy man, so our visits with him were infrequent. When he did make time for us, it was always a treat.

We stayed in New York for about a year. We went to school there, and I was baptized there. I was the only girl in a household of several boy cousins. We all loved one another and were very close, and lived like siblings. We fought and fussed at one another, but we always had each others' backs if anyone messed with any us. Even though I had gotten used to being there, I still looked forward to seeing my mother again.

Going to school in Rochester was not easy, especially as the newest kid in the class. Every day, my brother and I were picked on. The girls in my 4th-grade class bullied me, and many times, school kids chased us home.

One day, I returned home missing some of my braids. My cousin, Teresa, did my hair the entire time I was there. I was the daughter she always wanted but never had. She told me that if I came home running and/or missing any more braids, she would beat my butt, and I knew she meant it! Therefore, I had to stand up for myself and face those mean girls. And I did just that a short time later.

During recess one day, I was playing in the courtyard when about five of the mean girls surrounded me. They pushed and shoved me as if they wanted to fight. I was terrified! My heart thumped so loudly that I thought everyone around me could hear it. When other kids saw the commotion, they quickly surrounded me, chanting for us to fight. I thought back to another time when I ran home screaming while being chased. So, I closed my eyes and heard my mother telling me to fight back! I said a quick prayer, asking God for strength and courage to stand up to those girls and to win the fight.

All I can remember is beating up one of the girls so badly that, when I called out the other four, they didn't budge! Literally, no one stepped in the circle to fight me. From that moment on, I never had a problem with any of them again. All the fighting with my brother and cousin, Yoda, had paid off! They taught me how to be tough, and I was no longer afraid to defend myself physically (so I thought).

■ ■ ■

By the time we left New York, our mother had moved from Gary to South Bend, Indiana. She wasn't home the night we arrived, so my great-aunt took us over to my mother's friend's house, where we stayed until my mother came to get us the next day. I was ecstatic to see her and my little sister. While we were gone, my sister spent a lot of time at my mother's sister's house because of the trouble my mother had gotten herself into.

Her sister often helped my mother out financially and cared for us when there was no one else. I recall staying with my aunt and her family on a few occasions, because of my mother being incarcerated, or because she left us at home unattended for too long.

According to the National Resource Center on Children and Families of the Incarcerated (*https://nrccfi.camden.rutgers.edu/files/ nrccfi-fact-sheet-2014.pdf*), research shows that approximately 10 million children have experienced parental incarceration at some point in their lives. One in nine African American children (11.4 percent) in the United States have an incarcerated parent. While many of the risk factors children of incarcerated parents experience may be related to parental substance abuse, mental health, inadequate education, or other challenges, parental incarceration increases the risk of children living in poverty, or experiencing household instability independent of these other problems.

I was always grateful that my aunt cared so much about us. I admired her grace and her strong will. She had it together—a beautiful family of two children and a long-time husband, a great career, a beautiful home, and financial stability. She was the glue that kept her family together, and I wished we could have had her perfect life. She was living my dream of how a family should be. Staying with her was always a treat.

South Bend was supposed to be a fresh start and better life for us, but it was everything but that. The drugs, the poverty, the physical abuse between my mother and stepfather had only worsened. I had been anxious to come back to a drug- and alcohol-free home, and to a drug- and alcohol-free mom. The day after we returned home, I knew that was only a dream. Absolutely nothing had changed.

On our first day in South Bend, I was ordered to stay outside while my mother and others were inside getting high. The same thing happened in Gary. We hadn't even been back 24 hours, and here we were, facing the same mess as before. I remember being really upset with her.

In this new home, in this new neighborhood, I didn't know anyone. I had nothing to do but sit on the front step. When I was finally allowed to use the restroom, the kitchen was full of people and smoke and the same stench—an all-too-familiar smell—from previous times when my mother got high. And I knew about her weird actions afterwards, including the physical changes in her facial features.

It became easy for me to discern when she was high. The formation of her mouth was always one of the key indicators that she had been getting high, as was the sound of her voice, which changed when she was high from smoking crack. It was totally different from her normal voice.

I remember being so excited when my mother returned after she had been gone all day or evening, only to feel overcome with disappointment. Judging from the tell-tale signs that she was high, it was usually confirmed as soon as she opened her mouth to speak.

Between the ages of seven and nine, I knew far too much—*more than a kid my age should ever know*—about this home-wrecking substance called crack. I'd see burnt syringes from the sink filters, S.O.S. or Brillo pads used as part of the pipe, broken Bic ink pens used as the stem or straight shooter to smoke out of, empty Tylenol or aspirin bottles where the crack sat so the bottom could be heated with a lighter; the crack would then melt into a substance that was inhaled.

Seeing that my mother had not changed for the better was a devastating blow to me. It was like we were back in our Gary environment. The same patterns followed her to South Bend, only they seemed worse. All the time we were gone, I had high hopes that things would be different. She had sent us away for nothing!

Some nights I'd wake up to use the restroom or to get a drink, and the kitchen would be full of people smoking crack. My mother, and sometimes my stepfather, were in there somewhere.

Since we came back, it seemed like, every day, things became more unpredictable. One minute things were one way, and the next minute, they were different. One minute my stepfather was with us, the next, he wasn't. One minute my mother was home with us at night, the next, she was in jail and we were staying at her friend's place or my aunt's.

When I was around 8 and my brother was 10, we lived on the second floor of an apartment building. Often, we had to climb up to the roof to get into the house, because my mother left without making sure we could get in. Once he was on the roof, my brother climbed through the kitchen window, and opened the front door to let me in. Luckily, my sister was still at daycare at the time this usually happened. Just like in Gary, our utilities were periodically shut off for nonpayment, so the roof came in handy in more ways than one. If we didn't have electricity to refrigerate our food, we buried it in the snow on the roof to keep it frozen or cool.

Whenever our gas was turned off, I asked our neighbors across the street if I could use their kitchen to cook our food. Occasionally, I had to ask for water. They always said yes, but it was extremely awkward. The entire family silently stared as I used their appliances. I guess they were shocked that this eight-year-old girl lived like this. Hell, I'd be shocked, too!

One time, all we had to eat was pork and beans. I used our neighbor's stove to cook them, and, on my way home, the pot slipped out of my hands in the middle of the street. I picked up what was left, instantly overcome with sadness and grief. I felt so helpless. I was mostly concerned because there wasn't much of anything left to eat, and I was uncertain when my mother would be home again to feed us.

During times like these, I wished I was an adult so I could provide better for my siblings and me. It wasn't fair that we had to live in such conditions. Our main jobs should have been to get good grades and to keep our rooms clean, not to worry about where our next meal was coming from.

Sometimes, I'd watch my mother take meat out of our freezer with the intention of reselling it. I presume she did this to get money to buy drugs. One time, she took me with her—I didn't know where—but I was excited that she wanted me to go. Inside, I was all smiles that she wanted to spend quality time with me—*just me!*

My excitement was short-lived when we reached our destination—a convenience store. I quickly realized I was just a distraction in a shoplifting spree. She and a couple of her girlfriends used to "boost" (aka *steal*) merchandise and resell it for money, mainly used to buy drugs, but I also believe she did it to buy food. This particular night she wore a long, loose-fitting denim skirt. Underneath, she wore a girdle, where she stuffed all kinds of things. She put a huge box under her clothes that had a foot tub inside! I was shocked and terrified at the same time! I couldn't figure out how she could walk with all those things between her legs. To my surprise, she did!

I painfully realized that not only had she never intended for us to have quality time together, but I also wasn't as special as I had thought. I was simply a pawn and a lookout. It was like a fairy tale that went bad. I had a small part in the plot of the storyline. What a waste of hope that had been.

On another occasion, my mother was incarcerated for stealing or fraud, I'm not sure which, and my siblings and I had to stay with her sister. During our stay at my aunt's, I remember my cousin helped to get me ready for school one morning. She instructed me to remove my underclothes from the previous day and put on the fresh ones she handed me after I had washed up. I was in utter shock, because the ones I had on still looked clean.

I tried to keep the old ones on and explain it to her; to clear up the confusion. But she explained to me that people are supposed to change their underwear daily; then she made me take the new fresh pair. I remember thinking I had missed a memo, because I couldn't recall changing my underwear after one day. If they still looked clean, my mother had me wear them again, same as my clothes. At that moment, I felt like a peasant and beneath my cousin.

Clearly, our ways of living were different. At the age of eight, I was worried about how my own cousin perceived me. She meant no harm in giving me a lesson she hoped would stick with me long after we left their home. I was brought up wearing my clothes until they looked dirty. Her way was the "normal" way. Her family had the means to change into clean clothes every day. How cool was that! I did learn the lesson, and, from that moment on, I washed my underwear, by hand if I had to, to make sure I had clean underwear on each day.

Simple things like that gave me a better appreciation of life and helped me strive to do better. It may not have been a big deal to my cousin, but the epiphany I had that day allowed me to take control of my health, *regardless of my environment*. I would no longer deprive myself of clean underclothes if I could help it.

Children may become vulnerable when placed in frequently changing environments, because, at first, they lack familiarity and adaptability. Adjusting and learning new routines takes more time when children are hindered by fear. In time, they adjust. This was the case for me as I got acclimated every time we had to stay elsewhere, due to various circumstances. It was challenging in the beginning, but after a while, I got the hang of it.

Looking back, I learned to set attainable goals, regardless of where I was. To keep up with a constantly changing world, a person needs to be resilient and adaptable. These are essential qualities of life.

An important advantage for me in moving around so much was that it opened me up to learning new things. I learned different skills each time; skills that benefited my actual survival. I learned to develop a routine with each move, and I adjusted to my surroundings quicker. That way, I could help my siblings while they got acclimated. Keeping up with rapid changes equipped me for the vast changes that were yet to come.

As children, our experiences prepare us for our journey into adult life. For me, each move taught me that no matter where I was, I could still be at my best. I bounced back faster from good and bad situations. The constant transition made me eager for what lay ahead. I can honestly say now that I am not afraid of change, and that I eagerly welcome it. It's a way to grow.

Every move, every transition, and every challenge has made me stronger and wiser than I was before the previous move.

Key Takeaway from Chapter Three

Keep up with change.

More Takeaways...

- Resilience and adaptability to change are critical and can be life-saving.

- Learn your surroundings, in case of emergency, if you or your loved ones need to escape to safety, such as to a neighbor's house, community service center, or nearby family or friends.

- Make necessary adjustments quicker as life changes, so you are better prepared to handle the unexpected.

- Always keep this in mind: No matter where you are, you can still be at your best.

- Each change will make you stronger than the previous one.

FOUR

Round and Round We Go

Old habits die hard, or hardly die. That may be easier said than done, because some may not understand how deeply rooted the habit may be. Some of the habits we pick up are what we see when growing up, starting with the people we are closest to. This cyclical affect, *hence, round and round we go*, happens particularly in communities around the world where poverty and unstable households are prevalent.

Poverty, drugs, single-parent households, and lack of education plague our society in the inner cities and urban communities, where there are fewer resources, more so than in suburban areas or rural towns. Young people adapt to their surroundings by seeing and doing—*basically imitating*—what is going on around them. It becomes second nature as they grow into adulthood, only to pass down what they've seen to the next generation. The chances of repeating the same patterns are greater because there are no other options to take their place. It's all they know.

Young people may come to believe that this way of life is *the only way of life*. Very few distinguish between the good and the bad. Very few keep their surroundings from affecting them. Very few dare to be different. They may fear how they will be perceived if they don't live "the norm." They may also fear rejection from loved ones or members of the community.

Choosing to be different may cause envy from others, or it may make these young people a target. Developing confidence and an open mind to overcome the adversity might pave the way for others.

It may open the door to "opportunity" that others have been waiting for to make a difference in their lives or their community.

Being different should never discourage individuals from doing what is right or better for themselves and their loved ones.

■ ■ ■

After living in South Bend for a year or so, following my mom's unsuccessful attempt at making our lives better, she decided to follow my stepfather to Minnesota.

We arrived by Greyhound on August 5, 1989. It was my brother's 12th birthday, and I was 10 years old at the time. We stayed a short while with my mother's family on Vincent Avenue in North Minneapolis, until my mother found us another place to live. My stepfather stayed elsewhere during this time.

My mother couldn't find a place within a reasonable amount of time, so we ended up in 410 Shelter, a shelter for women and children in downtown Minneapolis. The shelter was packed. We stayed about a month before my mother found a place in North Minneapolis on the corner of Golden Valley Road.

Our home was near the family we had originally stayed with, right in the heart of a drug and poverty zone. My mother eventually met other drug-addicted people in the neighborhood, and she maintained relationships with others she met in the shelter, as well.

Coincidentally, my grandmother's sister, one of her many sisters, lived directly across the street from us. She was one of my favorite people. We frequently visited her, and it was a joy every time.

I remember one day when my mother and I stopped by. We were sitting at the dining room table when my great-aunt started sharing memories of my grandmother. I vividly recall that one of the conversations left my mother upset and weeping.

My great-aunt told stories of how my grandmother was physically abused at the hands of my grandfather, and she believed the abuse contributed to my grandmother's sudden, terminal illness.

My mother was distraught and very sad after hearing this. She had heard of the abuse between my grandparents, but she hadn't let it cloud her judgment or let it change how she loved her father. I think she wanted to give her dad the benefit of the doubt. He wasn't perfect, but she loved him for who he was.

My grandmother passed away from a brain aneurism when my mother was only two weeks old. My grandfather raised all five of their kids on his own, until he remarried. I can't imagine what it was like to raise five kids back then as a single father. My grandfather drank excessively, and sometimes became very violent and abusive. I think some of my mother's issues stemmed from those times. I remember when we visited him, he and my mother always fussed at each other. I truly believe it was because they were alike in so many ways.

Although my mom's sister provided maternal support while she was growing up, I don't believe it ever filled the void left when her mother passed away. As a child, I didn't understand all of this. I didn't understand how *her* childhood could have been the root cause of *our* own tumultuous childhood. What I did understand was that the way we lived was not fit for children, and that I would never raise my family under those same conditions.

My stepfather also came back into the picture and lived with us, off and on. During those times, our kitchen became the designated place to get high, just as it had been in Indiana. It became the norm on payday and on the first of the month when welfare recipients, like my mother, received their benefits from the government.

■ ■ ■

In 4th grade, I became very ill and was out of school for about a week. My mother said I was having a nervous breakdown. I had no clue, at the time, what that meant. I suffered with fever, chills, headache, sore throat, canker sores, weakness, and dizziness. No one else in the house had these symptoms. I felt emotionally and physically drained and didn't want to move, speak, or function anymore. I had become fed up with living this way; my 10-year-old body had been through the ringer, and it was giving out on me.

I was tired of being forced to live in substandard conditions, living in a drug zone, going without, and seeing my mother waste her life away using drugs, being abused by men, or abusing us when she became drunk and irate. I was tired of never knowing when and if there would be an end to this madness.

I couldn't go another 10 years like this. Hell, I didn't want to go another 10 minutes. My life should have been filled with fantasies of Cinderella and Snow White, not the responsibility of policing my mom so she wouldn't get high or intoxicated. I became weak and couldn't control how my body was reacting to these emotional stressors.

My mother took me to the doctor, who attributed my condition to stress.

I remember leaving Hennepin County Medical Center (HCMC) and stopping by Burger King while we waited for the bus. It was nice to be the center of my mom's attention for once in my life. I finally had some alone time with mommy and it was great. But that feeling of hope and happiness was sadly short-lived as we returned home. It was the same thing, just a different day.

Eventually, I hated living there. Our home and neighborhood were full of crime and poverty. Several homes were like mine, where crack smokers congregated in kitchens to get high. Unfortunately, the families and kids I played or visited with had become immune to what went on, and got along as if it was a normal part of life.

It was very peculiar to me why I couldn't conform and just be okay with it, too. It seemed like I was the only one who thought it was wrong to live this way, and the only one it mentally and physically affected, then and all my life. I wish it didn't have as much control over me, but, for some reason, I was never okay with it.

We moved from that North Minneapolis poverty-stricken, drug-infested neighborhood to one just like it in South Minneapolis.

The people, mostly guys, who sold drugs to my mom and others were guys I knew and grew up with.

I had to switch schools in the first trimester of 5th grade, due to our move. During my first year at Laura Ingalls Wilder Elementary and junior high school, it was mentally tough for me. I was very mean and angry, extremely belligerent and explosive, and, unfortunately, I took it out on those around me. No one was exempt. I mouthed off to my teachers, and got into a lot of physical fights, mostly with boys. I cursed out several faculty members, including the principal. I didn't know him, and he didn't know me. I was angry. I spent a lot of time in the behavioral room where kids who were misbehaving in class went to reflect on their actions. It got so bad that the staff in the behavior room didn't know how to handle me or the problems I was having.

It's not like I had preplanned having a bad day at school; it just happened. I'm not sure what came over me to act in this manner, but when it did, I did not use any damage control. I was angry, and couldn't pinpoint one specific thing that caused it. I was mad at the world for the way my life was going. Although no one at school was at fault, I took it out on them. At the time, I didn't know of any constructive ways to channel my anger or frustration, so it came out in my belligerent behavior.

I was fortunate to not have been expelled. My behavior definitely warranted it. The most the principal ever did was suspend me for a couple of days. My mother was required to come in and talk to him before I could return.

I felt ashamed and disappointed afterwards when these incidents happened. I wasn't pleased with myself, and I was remorseful for the way I had treated people who were simply trying to help me. I felt broken inside, and I broke everything I came into contact with, too. At the tender age of 11, I was on the path to self-destruction.

I hated when my mother had to come to my school and reinstate me after a suspension. She had to speak to the principal about my misbehavior and talk about ways to prevent it from happening again. I was ashamed of how she looked, and dreaded being seen with her. Many times, her face was disfigured from being beaten by my stepfather after one of their drunken tirades.

One time, she was in really bad shape. Her lip—she'd gotten stitches—was so swollen that it stood out at least two inches from her face. Her eye was blackened. As I watched my stepfather do it, it felt like we were in a scene from a horror movie.

I remember that fight all too well. They were drinking with friends across the hall. They spent a lot of time over there getting drunk or high, or both. I'm not sure what triggered the fight, but I heard a lot of commotion coming from outside our apartment. When I opened the door, I saw my stepfather punching my mom as if she was another man. Then I saw him take an empty Red Rose liquor bottle and bust her in the face. It was awful. I was sick to my stomach as I screamed and cried for my mom. I felt so sorry for her and I felt helpless, because I couldn't do anything to help her.

This kind of thing went on throughout my primary school years, and I had more fights at school and more trips to the behavior room and principal's office. Sometimes, I bypassed the behavior room and was sent straight to the principal's office. I could tell he was tired of seeing me sitting outside his office, because sometimes he made me wait for a long time.

The principal had an assistant whose desk was right outside his office door. She was a beautiful person, inside and out. She was always so kind to me, even when I didn't deserve it. Oftentimes, she'd talk to me as I waited. She wanted to help with whatever the situation was. She always encouraged me to do better the next time. I didn't understand why she cared so much, but she did. It was as if she could identify with what I was going through. She gave me hope, and I looked forward to seeing her on both good and bad occasions. It was a breath of fresh air talking to her. I used to wish she was my aunt and would get custody of us.

Talking with her gave me hope that I *could* change for the better and turn things around. She helped shape me into a better student each day I was there. I only wish I had told her, when I had the opportunity, how much of a difference she made in my life. Her compassion and humility made me feel loved and cared about. I felt obligated to show her I'd been listening and that I could do better.

Things at home hadn't gotten any better. In fact, they had worsened. Abuse and altercations continued in my mother and stepfather's tumultuous relationship. A lot of times, it took place in our apartment, or the neighbor's apartment across the hall.

The physical abuse against my brother and me also continued when my mother became excessively drunk and disorderly. At one point, I started fighting back, so I wouldn't be seriously injured. She physically jumped on us as if we had wronged her. It was like she was taking all her frustration and anger out on us.

Fortunately, it was just my brother and me, and not our little sister. My mother must have been conscious enough not to hurt her; however, it ended up hurting her, anyway, because she could see what my mother was doing to my brother and me.

One evening, my mother came home drunk from God knows where. I had one of my friends over who had planned to stay overnight. We were watching television, minding our own business, laughing and playing, doing what young girls did at our age. My mother hadn't been home long before she started yelling and becoming belligerent. She started fighting with me and hitting me uncontrollably.

I tried to get away from her, but she kept grabbing hold of me. I couldn't stop her from hitting me, so I ran and picked up a hammer, the first thing I could find. All at the same time, I was so hurt, scared, and angry that I almost hit my mother with the hammer. I screamed as I caught myself waving it over her head. I dropped it and ran out of the house, taking my friend and my sister with me.

First, we walked about three miles, at night, to take my sister to her father who was living then with a girlfriend. I don't remember where I went after dropping her off, but I did not go back home that night.

Here I was, a mere 11 years old, running away from home, because it was unsafe to be there. I wasn't running away for selfish adolescent reasons. I was running away so I could stay alive, or prevent myself from doing something I would regret. I loved my mother, and I would never have intentionally hurt her; but, in a split second, I could have seriously hurt her out of pain, anger, fear, and self-defense. What was even sadder is that she had ingrained in me to fight back and protect myself, no matter what. I just never would have imagined that, one day, I would be forced to use her advice against her.

I decided to write about the things that were going on in my life, and how I felt in general. My life was full of darkness and sadness all the time, and it was becoming extremely difficult to manage. I had no one to talk to, to let out some of these feelings.

After I finished writing whatever came to mind, I turned it in to my teacher. I didn't want anything from her, nor did I expect to be graded for it. I just wanted to get things off my chest, and writing about it was the first thing that came to mind. Directly asking for help wasn't my intent, but, deep down perhaps, I did hope for help—and change.

After my teacher read my paper, I remember her comforting me and asking if there was anything she could do. Before I knew it, the entire school faculty had read my paper, and they were extremely supportive of me. They even gave me a partial scholarship to MacPhail Center for Performing Arts for clarinet lessons, since I played in our school band.

I really enjoyed playing in the band, but I could have used a few more lessons. It was hard to practice at home, so the only time I could play was during band.

I was on my second clarinet because my first one disappeared from home. My gut feeling told me that my mother had something to do with its disappearance, but she denied it, as she did when other valuable things—clothes, money, or jewelry—came up missing. She tried to convince me I had misplaced it or lost it, but I was certain she took it and sold it for drugs. We couldn't leave anything of value in sight. If she thought she could sell something and make a profit to buy drugs, she did it. It saddened me that I couldn't trust my own mother, and that I couldn't get too relaxed in my own home and leave things out. I always hid my valuables or kept them elsewhere.

Although the bad seemed to outweigh the good, we did have good times with my mother, and as a family. When she was sober and clean, she was the coolest person to be around.

I used to try to make her laugh by being silly, because it's one thing she enjoyed when she was clean. Sometimes she was amused by the slightest things and laughed hysterically. When she got together with two of her siblings, the three of them would laugh up something fierce. I loved to see and hear her laugh, so I wanted to help with that as much as I could. I really enjoyed the sound of her laughter.

My mother had a great appreciation for good humor, and laughter came easily for her. Anyone who made her laugh automatically became one of her favorites. I recall wanting a video camcorder for my 13th birthday. She had psyched me into believing she was going to get one for me.

When my birthday finally came, she had a huge box waiting for me to open. Several of my friends were over, and I had told them all about the camcorder beforehand.

I opened the box, dug through the paper on top, only to find a toy video camcorder at the bottom. I was so humiliated, but, at the same time, it was hilarious. Everyone laughed hysterically; my mother was the worst of them all. She was so tickled that she never let me live it down, even years later.

During the not-so-funny times, we did our best to maintain. On the days my mother was sober, she was the typical mother who made the best of what we had. Life wasn't so bad during those times.

I would have given anything to keep it that way, but, unfortunately, those days didn't last.

As soon as she had the money to buy drugs or alcohol, it was back to the same old havoc. Sadly, if I had to pick a poison, I would have chosen drugs. I know it sounds bad and I prefer neither, but, when she got high, she wasn't abusive. In fact, she was the complete opposite. We could get away with practically anything, because she either didn't want to be distracted from smoking crack, or she would be too high to pay us any attention.

When she smoked crack, I didn't have to worry about falling asleep in fear of being beaten awake. When she was high on drugs, it was a much calmer atmosphere, as if we were nonexistent. She would often be paranoid and pace, looking out of the window, as if looking out for someone or something. It wasn't her normal behavior, but I'd take this any day over beatings.

One morning, my sister, brother, and I were home by ourselves. A friend of mine had stayed overnight. My mom had stayed out all night.

Later that morning, my mother came home with a guy friend she frequently hung out with. Theirs wasn't a personal or serious relationship, just someone she got high and drunk with.

On this particular morning, it appeared she was still drunk. We were all in the back room when she came in, drunken and disorderly. She started in on my brother and me, but he got it the most. He was sitting on the radiator, while they went back and forth verbally. Her friend made several attempts to calm her down, to no avail.

She relentlessly went after my brother. I remember my brother appearing so defenseless as he tried to reason with her. We were all perplexed at why she was so outraged with us that morning. She hadn't been home 20 minutes, and she was already going crazy on us.

Things eventually turned physical. I felt helpless that I couldn't get her off my brother. Before I could look up, my mother had grabbed hold of the broom and lunged towards him. As he defended himself, she rammed the broom handle down his throat with all her might, knocking his front teeth to the back of his throat!

My brother screamed in pain and agony as he jumped up off the radiator. Blood went everywhere, my baby sister was screaming, and I was screaming and out of my mind by now.

This felt so much like a bad dream. I wished and prayed that, when I woke up, the dream would all be over, but it wasn't.

I don't remember what happened next, or in what order. All I know is that I ended up at the hospital. My friend was still with me, just as shocked and disbelieving as I was. I was in the room with my brother, and then they took him off to surgery.

I was broken beyond repair, at this point. I was deeply hurting for my brother. I loved him so much, and it hurt me that I couldn't protect him the way he had always protected my sister and me. My brother was about 13 years old at the time. He didn't deserve this, nor did he do anything to warrant it.

I was terrified of being in the emergency room with the doctors and social workers, and I couldn't stop shaking. Next thing I heard was my mother's voice. She was loud and disorderly, crying, and asking for my brother. Her friend had brought her to the hospital, and he looked sad as well. He was again trying to calm her down so people could talk to her. Moments later, the surgeon came out.

I'll never forget the look of disgust and disdain on his face as he beckoned to the police to take her away when she walked up to him.

Right before my eyes, my mother was handcuffed and hauled off by the police. I cried and screamed, because I didn't want her to go away. I was so out of it I can't recall where my sister was during this time. Then, everything went dark for me. I just wanted to fade away from this.

My family, who was all I had and whom I loved dearly, was being taken away from me, one by one, in different directions. I was lost and didn't know what to expect next.

From that moment, I felt my life couldn't get any worse. I could not fathom what would cause my mother to put us in this kind of danger. I didn't understand why she couldn't control her actions, and why she couldn't break this vicious cycle of substance and physical abuse.

Since my stepfather was, for the most part, out of the picture now, it was a perfectly good time to clean up her act, because she was no longer under his influence.

Matters were out of my control now. There was nothing I could do to help my siblings and myself. It was unclear what lay ahead for us—a daunting feeling.

■ ■ ■

Stress takes a toll on our bodies in numerous ways. It's best to address the issues causing stress to prevent it from going to the extreme. Children living in dysfunctional homes, or who are in temporary placement homes, suffer from anxiety and stress due to these living conditions, as well as pressures or responsibilities placed on them because of their environment or absentee parents.

They do not know about the help they can get to keep themselves healthy enough to fight another day. School faculty, church members, and mentors from the community are some of these great resources.

Growing up, I wish I had opened up more to someone at my school. Students experiencing trauma need and depend on our schools' faculties to care enough beyond the classroom. If there is any indication of an unhealthy or unsafe environment outside of school, they need to get involved on our behalf. For example, my constant misbehavior in school was my cry for help, and it may be the way other youth in similar situations cry out. I wasn't well, and neither were things at home.

My mother's appearance when she came to my school should have raised a flag that things weren't okay at home. It explained why I was having so much trouble in school. It's part of the schools' obligations as educators and guardians by day to take an interest in students' well-being and safety beyond school hours. Their interest and involvement can make a difference and save the lives of young people living in unhealthy conditions.

On the other hand, as students living with daily trauma at home, it's our obligation to ask for help when we need it. We shouldn't fear the consequences, because, in the end, we may not just be saving our own lives, but also the lives of our loved ones.

Unfortunately, some of the issues that go on in dysfunctional households or in poorer communities are generations old. Drug and alcohol abuse, poverty, and lack of education plague communities where resources are scarce, impeding better futures for many young people.

Children growing up in these environments think it is a normal way of life. A lot of them have no one on the outside to show them a better way, or teach them differently. It's not uncommon—in fact, chances are exponentially higher—for problems, such as literacy challenges, addictions, violence, and abuse, to become patterns that will repeat in yet another generation.

To break the cycle and improve lives, communities, and future generations, we need to become accountable and make it our duty to make better choices and help others do the same. We've seen, first-hand, the results and consequences of these patterns of behavior—even more reason to push ourselves to not repeat the sins of our past. We're ultimately responsible for taking control of our own destiny and not allowing ourselves to be influenced by our surroundings. We may not be able to control others' actions, but we <u>can</u> *control how we let their actions affect our lives, short-term and long-term.*

It's not always easy to be different, to choose better, especially when only a few others in our surroundings do so. Self-governing, not being influenced by others, takes a lot of courage and willpower. It can cause others to become jealous or envious of us, which can be discouraging, at times. We can't let it derail us from our plans for improving our lives. I experienced, first-hand, what this felt like.

I was driven to seek a better education and better options for myself, and others treated me differently; sometimes good and sometimes not so good. With more education, I saw things in a new light, and made smarter choices. There were people I grew up with or who lived in the same community as me who perceived it as if I thought I was better than them. I wasn't doing anything they couldn't do, but, for some reason, they made me out as the bad guy.

I've been told that I think I'm white or that I act white, just because my vocabulary or pronunciation is different than the majority of those from my neighborhood. I didn't think I was better than anyone else, I was simply being me, and making the best of the opportunities available to me. I was singled out or targeted and picked on, because they perceived me in a different way. It didn't make my journey easy. In fact, sometimes I found myself lowering my standards or dumbing myself down, just to fit in or avoid being singled out. Eventually, I got enough courage to accept that I am different because I chose different options.

I always told my peers that they, too, could change their lives for the better, just by pushing themselves a little harder. Whether or not they did so was no longer my concern. I wouldn't let their negativity prevent me from making a difference.

If people disliked me, that affirmed to me that I must be doing something right, and I could only hope that they might follow suit. Sometimes for others to believe, all it takes is one person to show that it can be done. I, too, was inspired by watching others, which motivated me to work hard at building a brighter future. I also experienced how people are more inclined to help you when they see you're trying to better yourself.

Key Takeaway from Chapter Four

Discern poor habits and break the cycle.

More Takeaways...

- Be aware of imitating others' poor habits.

- Dare to be *different*.

- Being different and standing out isn't a bad thing if it's for a positive cause.

- Never feel obligated to take on your loved ones' bad habits or poor choices.

- To break the cycle and improve your life, future generations' lives, and your communities, be accountable, make better choices, and help others do the same.

- We may not be able to control others' actions, but we *can* control how we allow their actions to affect our lives, now and in the future.

- With more education, I made smarter choices.

- Don't let others' perceptions keep you from making a difference.

- All it takes is one person leading the way for others to believe.

- *You* are that one person.

FIVE

Girls Only

Being taken from your family when you're young is not easy, and it causes distress. Enduring the circumstances that cause the separation is, in itself, traumatizing, but going to an unfamiliar place where you don't know anyone can make it even worse.

It's important that temporary placement facilities create programs or operating rhythms that focus on making the transition smoother for the young people staying there; programs that help them adjust to the changes and manage their emotions effectively, helping them feel that they're part of the *solution* and not the problem.

Creating these kinds of programs helps kids fit in right away. They help kids feel like they're in a home away from home, rather than in a place where they feel they've done something wrong. Surprisingly, temporary placement facilities with strict or more rigorous processes can make adjustment even more challenging, resulting in behavioral issues, or worse.

It would be so valuable for the young people placed in these establishments to be taught essential life skills they can apply during and after their stay, such as:

- Skills to help build them up and promote self-growth
- Skills that teach them the importance of studying and completing their school work
- Skills on how to effectively communicate their feelings

- Skills on how to recognize the importance of making better choices, so they don't end up repeating the same cycle of behavior that resulted in them being placed there.

Working closely with a mentor or advocate could go a long way in making their stay as productive as possible. Such guidance could, in fact, save a young person's life.

Speaking from experience, if I would have had a positive intervention like this, it would have helped me transition upfront, rather than feeling that I was being punished for something I had no control over.

It felt like I'd been sent to a detention center for children. But I hadn't forced my mother to do the things she did. Hell, on numerous occasions, I begged and pleaded with her *not to do those things*. Therefore, I didn't understand why I had to live in a place where I wasn't allowed to watch television unless I *earned* it. I was made to feel as though I had done something wrong.

My brother and sister and I were all placed in temporary living arrangements following the incident with my brother. I went to an all-girl group home in Golden Valley, Minnesota, while my sister went to live with her father, and my brother stayed with our uncle. I was sad that I was the only one placed in a facility, but there weren't many options for me as far as family.

This all-girl group home life was foreign to me. Other girls were there for reasons similar to mine, while others had gotten into trouble at home. I was one of the youngest. Those like me, who didn't have much control over what had put them there, seemed just as lonely as I was. While at the facility, they were in a better environment, but I couldn't help feeling they missed their mommies, too.

The girls who were there because of their own bad choices had a bad-girl demeanor.

I was so alone there and just wanted to go home to my family.

At first, I thought this stay would be short-term, temporary, and that I would be back home in a day or two. I thought that they were only keeping me there until my mother sobered up and my brother was out of the hospital.

A week went by, then another. After several months, I realized this might be long-term—or permanent!

It was hard adjusting to this different environment. The staff members were kind and understanding, for the most part—notably Les—but still, this was no place like home, surrounded by loved ones.

The system at the group home was different from what I was accustomed to. We had to earn levels of privileges, such as television, outdoors, and allowance.

When someone was first admitted, she automatically started at the lowest level and worked her way up. To me, it should have been the other way around, where everyone started on the same level, with all privileges, until they did something to lose them. This way, no one would have felt singled out. It may have shed light on the situation that put each of us there in the first place.

The rules of the home made me feel like we were divided. This made me feel inferior to the other girls, like I was being punished for having to come here, or for having bad behavior. Girls on different levels didn't associate much with the ones on lower levels having fewer privileges. We all could have felt more united if we had had the same privileges from the beginning of our stay. It caused tension among the girls. Instead of healing and coping with our situations, the division made us more contentious.

Had things been the other way with everyone starting with all privileges, my first few weeks would have been much easier. All I remember is feeling lonely and afraid at first, like I was in a faraway place where people go to get punished for doing something bad. I really missed my mother and my siblings, and sleeping in my own bed. It was extremely hard for me, and all I could think about was how much I missed my mommy. I prayed they wouldn't turn the lights out at night, because I was afraid of my thoughts. I used to wish it were all a dream and that my mother would burst through those doors to take me home.

But she never did.

To get promoted to the next level, we had to set and achieve attainable goals. The goals typically included completing chores, attending the in-house school for the 30-plus girls, and having generally good behavior.

My goals were a bit different from the norm. One specific goal was created by some of the staff members—to *stop whining*. Apparently, I whined excessively whenever I needed or wanted something, or when I became emotional.

Whining throughout my young life had been another form of expression for me. I didn't understand why it was such a big deal. It wasn't like I had control over it, or that I did it intentionally; it just happened sometimes. Needless to say, this goal was challenging for me and, quite frankly, unrealistic. However, I gave it my best shot.

Grades in the in-house school ranged from junior high to high school; most of the girls were in high school. I was the youngest and among the few in junior high.

After attending one of the classes, which were taught by "certified teachers," I pleaded with my social worker to allow me to continue attending public school at Laura Ingalls Wilder. I knew I should be doing far more challenging work in 7th grade than what they were teaching in-house, and I was not going to allow this system to thwart me from getting a better education.

The state approved my attending public school, and they issued me monthly bus passes and tokens to get to and from school.

The commute took about three hours each way, and I had to walk two miles to reach the nearest bus stop. That meant I had to get up by 5:00 a.m. each morning, and be out the door no later than 5:30 a.m.

It was brutal during the winter months. I had to walk in several feet of snow and in below-zero weather, if I wanted a better education than what the shelter provided. I remember the expression on the night shift person's face as I headed out each morning. She looked amazed at my determination and willpower. Sometimes, she offered me a ride to the bus stop, usually when it was brutally cold. I was extremely grateful for her kindness.

I'm not a big fan of nature and darkness in deserted places, so at the age of 11, being outside alone in the early morning darkness was terrifying for me. I worried about animals and humans getting me. I prayed each day as I walked my route, and held my head up to God. That is the only way I made it safely and sanely each day.

The endless support from my teacher, Mr. Bess; hall monitor/ disciplinary advisor, Mr. Davis; and principal, Mr. Smith, helped me get through school and stay focused during this time. They were a vital part of my support system, and I really appreciated them. Their unconditional love and support allowed me to have peace of mind while I was at school.

I truly believe they sympathized with what I was going through at home. They saw my struggle. They had seen my mother and the condition she was in on those occasions when she had to visit me at school. They could figure out that things at home weren't conducive to my getting a good education. I believe they were inclined to help me and not be so quick to write me off, because they saw me persevere each day, as I tried not to let my situation take me off course.

It was rough in the beginning. But they gave me chances, worked with me, and did not give up on me. I realized I had to try harder.

My behavior improved, and I was less confrontational and combative. My demeanor and attitude improved as they helped me see that I could make a difference with my life. Their inspiration and words of encouragement helped me to believe I could excel, regardless of what was going on at home.

Because of them, I didn't have to think much about what my

life was going to be like once the bell rang at the end of the day. I could stay focused without worrying about anything that was going on in my life at the time.

I enjoyed class and learning, and I looked forward to being with the friends I had made at school. They were like my second family.

Attending school away from the shelter was therapeutic, and it helped to take my mind off things. It was the only form of normalcy I had, at the time. I could be an 11-year-old in junior high.

I often cried as I rode the bus, thinking about my family and where they were. I was mostly concerned about my sister, who was living with her father. My biggest concern was my stepfather's own substance abuse issues. He was an alcoholic, crack addict, and heroin addict.

His house, at the time, was along the bus route I rode every day.

I only had a limited time to be away from the shelter before I was reported missing, but enough time to stop over and visit my sister as often as I could.

After our first visit, I realized this was harder to deal with than not seeing her at all. She was alone most of the time, while my stepfather was in another room getting high or intoxicated. She would be so happy to see me, just as I was elated to see and hug her. From the moment I walked in the door, I never wanted to leave her. Time went by so fast, and it just wasn't enough.

When it came time for me to go, she was sad and I was an utter mess. Nothing in the world could be worse than the pain I felt each time I left my sister. I missed this little girl so much and wanted to be with her, protecting her from all harm and negligence. Although her father loved her, he was sick himself and couldn't give her the love and nurturing that she needed as a little girl. I freaking missed her.

I felt sad as I rode back to the shelter after seeing her. I'd put my head down so others wouldn't see me crying. Sometimes, I cried myself to sleep, and I missed my exit stop.

I thought about taking her or staying there with her and not returning to the shelter, but I knew that would just make matters worse. I knew I had to let it play out in court, but I just wanted my sister to know that she could count on me and that I would be back for her soon. Unfortunately, she eventually was taken away from her father and put into a foster home, because he received multiple DWIs while she was in his custody.

I lived in the all-girl shelter for seven or eight months before I was transferred somewhere else. I probably would have stayed there for the duration, but one day appeared to be more challenging for me than others, and I ended up in a juvenile facility. I guess I was getting restless and tired of being away from my family. It had been months since I last spoke to my mother, and I wasn't sure when I'd talk to her next. Separated from my siblings, I basically had no one.

Things were becoming more than I, an 11-year-old, could handle. I'd been able to mostly suppress my feelings and frustrations and manage my stress, but this one day had gotten the best of me.

I wanted my mother, or at least to talk to her, but the staff would not allow me to because of a court order that I could have no contact with her. I had no idea why, so I pouted and threw fits throughout the day.

That same day, I threw a small decorative couch pillow at one of the staff members. It barely made contact with her. She called the police and they arrived in minutes. I was terrified, so I ran and hid under a bed. I could hear everyone searching for me for about 20 minutes before they found me. They put me in the back seat of the police car and took me to downtown Minneapolis to a juvenile detention center. I spent a couple days there before I was transferred to a foster home.

I lived in the foster home for several months. It was okay at first, because it was the family of a couple of friends from school.

Several months later, I witnessed the caregiver abusing one of the other foster kids. I reported the incident to my caseworker, and I was removed from the home. I was then transferred to another group home for girls in South Minneapolis, where I stayed for a short stint. I was then moved to another children's shelter not far away.

Key Takeaway from Chapter Five

Home away from home.

More Takeaways . . .

- Temporary placement facilities can play an important role in children's and youth's smooth transition by making it a home away from home.

- Children and youth need programs that help them feel they are a part of the solution and not the problem.

- Providing advocacy can help make a positive difference in their stay.

- Temporary placement facilities should create an environment of equality to minimize division among the children and youth.

- Staff should pay attention to signs of distress when interacting with children or youth, as it may be a cry for help.

- Educators play a pivotal role in providing support to students during a time of transition and hardship.

- Educators' words of encouragement helped me believe I could still excel, regardless of what went on at home.

- It's important to inspire children and youth during their time at temporary placement facilities to stay the course, as things will get better with time.

SIX

Co-ed Group Home

This place was different from the other group homes where I had lived. It was co-ed, with boys and girls in the same unit. It was about 20 times bigger and had kids of all ages, ranging from newborns to 17-year-olds. Each unit, referred to as a hall, was divided into age groups. I was in the hall for kids between 10 and 15 years old. The rooms had two beds, and most of us had roommates, whether we liked it or not.

The facility had different activity rooms and amenities.

Unit staff members were mostly in their 20s or early 30s, and had a background or education in youth development. Most of them were pretty fun, laid back, and relatable, which made the adjustment somewhat easier. I interacted with the staff and other kids in my hall, but I spent a lot of time alone, in my room, where I preferred to be.

I found more peace being alone in my room away from the chaos. Isolation was my safe haven while I was there. It was just easier that way, considering the number of kids and their issues. Kids would act out because of things going on in their lives, and, as a result, they developed behavioral issues.

One of my most difficult challenges while living there was how close the shelter was to my family home before we were taken away. It was the neighborhood I was most familiar with, and where all my friends still lived. So many times, I wanted to run away and go home, but I knew that no one would be there. My mother was in treatment somewhere, and my brother and sister lived in different places, as well.

I wished I could convince the state that I was mature and capable enough of raising my sister and brother. Although I was only 12 years old, I would promise the state I would get good grades and make sure my sister and brother did, too. I would protect them and care for them like a mother should. I would promise the court my siblings would never again be hurt. It would be just the three of us until our mother got better.

I knew I could do it, but I needed to convince the judge. After all, what could be so difficult about caring for your loved ones?

■ ■ ■

A year or so after the incident with my brother, my mom finished her time in jail and rehabilitation, then we were released back home to her care. However, she was still on probation and had to undergo regular drug testing as part of her release and custody arrangements.

We were all finally back together again, and I could not have been happier. I was hopeful that things would stay this way. Finally, we had the sober and nurturing mother I had longed for most of my life. I basked in her sobriety, love, and affection.

My life was great during this time. I didn't want it to end, but, unfortunately, it did. Mommy gradually relapsed. She started with marijuana again, and crack soon followed, despite her being on probation and having drug screenings.

Even though she was clearly aware that she risked losing us again, it didn't stop her from getting high. She chose drugs over being there for us; she chose drugs over protecting us from going into the homes of strangers, again. I was extremely disappointed and hurt, sad, and angry that we were going back down the same road of catastrophe. I worried about it all the time.

As before, I would plead with her not to get high. All I would get in return were lies, saying she would stop; the same old lies I'd heard in the past every other time she relapsed. I should have known it was too good to be true: to be able to come home from school and have a sober mother there waiting for us; to not have to wake up in the middle of the night to a smoky, stinky kitchen full of crackheads getting high; to be able to sleep at night and not wake up to a beating. I should have known it was only a hoax. I didn't want to live that life again or be taken away, because, Lord knows, I wouldn't be able to handle it. She had promised me that she wouldn't do this again, or put us through what we had just gone through.

It was only a matter of time before we would be taken away.

When she went for her required drug screenings, her urine samples were far from clean—that is, if she used her own pee. At first, it didn't dawn on me why she asked us to urinate in a cup for her. I didn't question it because she was my mother, and maybe it was a part of her motherly duties to make sure our pee was healthy. Well, apparently, she would stash one of our urine samples in her clothes and take it into the bathroom while being tested.

The crazy part is, when you're screened for drugs, typically a lab worker or officer escorts you to the restroom. How she pulled it off is beyond me, but, for a while, she did. When I realized what she was using our urine for, I refused to do it, I would no longer lie for her, or let her use me to cover her poor choices.

She eventually stopped asking me, and mostly went to my sister or brother for their urine. One day she got caught and had to go back to rehab. We were again separated.

My brother, sister, and I had been bounced around to foster homes, group homes, and/or family members' homes due to my mother's drug relapses and probation violations. One time, my brother went to New York to live with our father's side of the family, my sister went to a foster home, and I was sent to a group home.

The foster home where my sister was placed had me concerned. I remember her being sent to bed as early as 7:00 p.m. in the summer, when it was still sunny and kids were outside playing. I vaguely recall something wasn't right with that family, and she was removed from their home. She then bounced around to other foster homes until she ended up with her godparents, where she was better taken care of than in any of the other homes she had gone to.

Knowing that she had to go through this while I was stuck in another group home made me feel helpless and like a failure. I tortured myself thinking about her and what she may have been going through. The thought that she might be scared or hurt frightened and hurt me, as well. At the time, it was literally one of the most painful things I'd ever had to bear. I'd rather be beaten and live in a drug-infested home than have my sister go through this.

I couldn't understand why this was happening to us. It wasn't helping us; it was hurting us even more. It was worse than being taken away from home. I just wanted my sister to know that she could count on me, and that I would be back for her soon.

During my stay in the South Minneapolis children's group home, I was again cut off from communicating with my mother during her failed attempts at sobriety. Once again, it seemed that I had no one. I did my best to keep my predicament from causing me to mentally deteriorate. The loneliness and emptiness of not having my family weighed heavily on me. At one point, I felt I was a ticking time bomb.

■ ■ ■

Often, people take for granted the privilege of having loved ones nearby. We don't realize how important they are and the role they play in our lives until we no longer have them. In times like this, we must appreciate even their imperfections, and love them for who they are. Naturally, we believe they will always be there. We don't think seriously that, someday, things may change.

Going through these separations helped me realize how important family really is. Everyone needs someone to love, to talk to, or to just be there for them. I longed to have their love present in my life again.

■ ■ ■

In my hall, I could relate to and open up to one particular staff member. We had mature conversations about what was going on in my life, and how I could manage these issues positively.

Talking to this person was comforting, because he didn't view me as just a kid who had been taken away from home, or someone who had parental issues. He was understanding and easy to talk to. He was outgoing and down to earth, a person I could confide in. Our relationship was different from relationships with other staff members.

Over several months, our relationship grew. It was as though we had known each other for years. He would come to my room when I was there alone, and talk with me about anything. We had no boundaries or differences between us. He talked to me like I was someone his age. It was refreshing, considering I had no one else I could talk to. Whenever I was having a rough day, I would talk to him, and somehow it all got turned around and would be okay.

Although there was a tremendous age difference (I was 12 and he was 24), it was irrelevant to the relationship we had formed. Our conversations and relationship matured. Before long, I was finding ways to meet with him outside of the group home.

I used my outside passes to visit him in his home, a studio apartment, bordering downtown and South Minneapolis near the bus route. These visits were new for me, and I didn't want them to end. Now I had someone who seemed to care about me and who helped take my mind off the pain and emptiness of being away from my family. I felt safe with him, and I trusted him.

Living at the group home gave me a sense of security. I no longer felt alone. I felt more secure there, because I trusted that he would protect me from whatever I feared. It was similar to how I felt when I was home and my mother was sober. During those times, she played her role well in making us feel secure, and making sure we were taken care of. Her presence was so comforting that I didn't want to be in any other place. I experienced this same feeling, this peace of mind, when he was around.

I knew that he wasn't supposed to take this kind of interest in me while he worked in the group home, so I kept it to myself. I would act as I normally acted (keeping to myself and not paying him much attention) when we were amongst the other residents and staff.

He had a one-year-old son at the time. His son lived with the mother, whom he was no longer with. I visited on the weekends, or sometimes during the week before I went back to the home after school.

Our relationship went on for several months, even after I was discharged from the home and released back into my mother's custody. The more time we spent together, the more comfortable I felt. He made me feel like I really mattered.

Things got real for me one evening. It was an intimate evening, at first. We listened to music, and we kissed. One thing led to another and, before I knew it, we were lying in his sleeping area, face-to-face, body-to-body. Mentally, I knew what was about to take place, but my body wasn't ready for it. I couldn't stop shaking. I was terrified.

I realized I had been brave and mature throughout our entire relationship, but I was not prepared for this whole other level that I hadn't had time to get ready for. I did my best to hide my nervousness to keep up with him.

I remember lying on his bed, jumping at every noise I heard. I was a wreck. All I could think about was, when will this be over? It was very painful, and I didn't enjoy it one bit. Afterwards, we didn't speak much, other than him checking to see if I was okay. I pretended I was fine and that I enjoyed our time together.

When he took me home, I remember I was barely able to keep my balance. My legs shook badly, and they were extremely sore. I didn't know how to make it stop. I was hoping and praying he wouldn't notice. While walking through the hallway to go to his car, I hugged the wall so that I could support myself, in case I lost my balance.

When we neared my place, I got out on the corner of my block and walked the rest of the way. I walked in the door as if nothing had happened. This became routine and easier as time went on.

It was nice being home again with my mother and sister. My mom had completed her drug rehabilitation program and was sober again. She found a nice townhome in South Minneapolis, and life was going well for us. My brother had gotten into trouble and had to stay in an all-boys' home. We frequently visited him in Blaine, Minnesota. He, too, was getting better at making choices.

During one of our visits, it occurred to me that my brother's roommate was the younger brother of the guy I was seeing. Ironically, this discovery came a couple weeks after my mother's dream about me dating a much older guy. She was enraged as she told me about the dream, and I could tell it really bothered her. She said that, in the dream, I had asked her if I could continue seeing him, and I'd begged her not to prosecute him. It was surreal.

As time went on, he and I talked and saw less of each other. Eventually, our relationship ended, and I never had contact with him again.

Except, one day, I saw him in a store. He was by himself. It had been years since I'd seen him. He looked at me as if he had seen a ghost. He didn't speak or greet me in any way. I didn't understand why he was being so standoffish, as if he didn't know me. A moment later, he vanished into thin air. I was perplexed and wondered if I had done or said anything wrong in the past.

■ ■ ■

Throughout my childhood, we moved quite a bit. Not long after settling in, it would be time to move again.

In the summer of my 12th year, I visited my family in Rochester, New York, for a few months. I went alone, as my brother stayed in Minnesota.

After my stay in Rochester, and on my way back to Minnesota, my brother met me in Gary, Indiana, where we visited our grandfather for a few days; then we caught the Amtrak home.

By this time, my mom had moved into a house in South Minneapolis, intending to buy it. She was doing very well and was enrolled in a HUD program.

When my brother and I arrived home, we went to our new home only to find that no one was there. It was early in the evening, so I had expected my mother would be there, because she knew we were coming.

As the day went by, there was still no sign of her or my sister. This was not a good sign, or at least not the sign I had hoped for.

Night came and we were still waiting on the porch. We ended up sleeping on the back porch until the next day, when she finally came home. I could tell she had been out getting high, and I was surprised.

There went my morale and my excitement at being back home. What had happened? She had been on the right track before I left for New York. She had a steady job, and she was in the process of buying a home. I couldn't figure out why she would risk losing it all again over drugs.

Soon, I learned that not much had changed and that she was back taking the occasional lethal combination of drugs and alcohol.

Only my sister and I were home one evening my mother had been drinking. She became drunk and belligerent, and fussed and screamed about any and everything. She would not leave me alone. She was taking her aggression and anger out on me, and I didn't know why. What had I done, or what had happened to piss her off to that extreme? I was tired of her badgering me.

As soon as I sensed that she was on the verge of becoming violent, I called 911. She was very hostile with them, and they handcuffed her and took her to a detox facility where she was kept overnight. My sister and I went to the same children's shelter in South Minneapolis where I had been before.

When we arrived, it was late. I was emotionally distraught,

and my sister seemed scared and confused. We remained in the intake unit for the rest of the night. By the grace of God, we hadn't been split up, which I had feared the most. We slept on a cot, and I watched over my sister as she fell asleep. I did my best to stay brave for her until she shut her eyes.

At this point, I felt defeated. I had done everything I could to protect my sister from places like this, but apparently my "everything" wasn't enough. I was numb. Although tears streamed from my eyes, I couldn't feel them. I cried for what felt like that entire night, as I clutched my sister and kept watch over her.

We were released a couple of days later, and we were all back home. I remember my mother was upset with me. She blamed me for what had happened. Maybe she would have preferred that I endure the inevitable, or that I would leave home on my own, instead of calling 911. I don't know. I just stayed clear of her for a while until things were right between us again.

Quite often, children and youth are taken advantage of during vulnerable times. Especially in situations where there is no parent or familiar family member. This is one of many examples of why it's extremely important that children and youth who have been removed from their homes have a mentor.

Teachers, principals, community members, and religious leaders can make a difference by coaching and providing positive and effective guidance to help children and youth get through the difficult days ahead.

My teachers, hall monitor/disciplinary advisor, and principal did that for me, as I moved from place to place. Their support helped me through my fears and other emotions. They encouraged me throughout, and their patience and understanding directly influenced my behavior and my will to improve.

They neither gave up on me nor wrote me off, as they very well could have. Their continual belief turned me into a believer and made me want to push myself even harder each day. Without their support, I don't know if I would have succeeded in keeping it all together. Although I felt I had the weight of the world on my shoulders, having them in my corner made a world of difference.

This same type of support would be just as beneficial in group homes or foster homes, so that children and youth wouldn't have to face these times alone.

Having someone to coach and guide a young person along the way can minimize behavioral issues, which frequently occur in such places. A lot of the behavioral issues are caused when no one is fully invested in the child. The child is often in the dark, and no one is explaining to them what is going on, or coaching them on how they can best get through it. Instead, they're handed a rulebook listing the do's and don'ts while staying there.

With proper protocols and parameters in place, staff and faculty members can form a healthy mentorship with the residents. These procedures should be designed to protect the staff member *and* the child from harm and unethical behavior.

It also helps in preventing situations like mine with the older male staff member from occurring. Some reasons why people are reluctant to mentor children and work with them one-on-one are the fear of accusations of unethical behavior, based on inappropriate behavior that may have occurred in the past, or being suspected of inappropriate behavior, or perhaps being falsely accused. In any situation, mentoring is challenging, but, with the right processes in place, mentoring can still be done effectively.

What I realize now that I didn't know then was, I was looking for affection, but in the wrong place. The love and affection I was longing for was not from a 24-year-old man, but perhaps from my mother and father. Our relationship was fictitious; this staff member had no intention of filling the void in my life at the time. I was vulnerable and couldn't distinguish between sincerity and selfish gain. I know now that I was too young to make that call. He overstepped the boundaries of interaction between an inappropriately aged person and an adolescent. As a vulnerable adolescent, I was put in an even more vulnerable position and was taken advantage of.

The ramifications of that relationship have made it difficult for me to trust others' intentions, and it has made me skeptical of being open and vulnerable with others. I fear they may not have my best interests in mind, or they may have a hidden agenda or ulterior motive.

If I could go back to that time, understanding what I now know, I would have been more emotionally aware of my feelings and actions, making sure I was engaging in only age-appropriate behavior.

I would also have confided in another adult about the things going on in my life, to get a different perspective and possibly genuine and effective help.

Key Takeaway from Chapter Six

Be emotionally aware of your vulnerabilities.

More Takeaways...

- Being vulnerable and stressed can negatively affect our choices.

- When feeling vulnerable, engage in age-appropriate situations and conversations.

- Confide in people you can trust to get a different perspective or proper guidance for handling situations you're uncertain of.

- By keeping a positive outlook during difficult times, I could prevent circumstances from getting worse.

- My mindset was that the current hardship was only temporary. Sometimes, this helped me manage my emotions so I wasn't feeling vulnerable or helpless.

SEVEN

Nine Months Later

Teen and adolescent parenting has become epidemic in urban communities over the last several decades. For various reasons, youth feel they are mature enough or ready to become parents. While numerous factors contribute to this upswing in teen parenthood, there appears to be a trending pattern in certain communities and environments.

Feeling ready for parenthood could stem from situations that make youth feel they're capable of taking on such responsibility. Maybe they're older than their true age, and already making adult-like decisions and choices.

Another reason is they have not been exposed to what is truly involved in parental responsibility, because they didn't see it in their own homes. They may have grown up where absentee parents were the norm, or the parent(s) they did observe may have lacked the adequate resources—such as having a job with substantial income—to care for a child.

These conditions could mislead the child, giving a false impression about effective parenting. As a result, a teenager may believe that, if the majority of the people in their community can have babies and raise them without resources and life's necessities, then why can't they?

Another factor contributing to why teens believe parenthood is easy is that they may have had to raise their siblings or other children while growing up. Consequently, they feel they have enough experience that qualifies them to be parents. Often, in communities where resources are scarce and poverty is high, teens and youth are left to take care of themselves or other children while their absentee parents are dealing with substance abuse problems, childhood issues, or lack of appropriate childcare while they're working. The consequence of children raising themselves is that the child is now open to making poor choices, including having premature sex.

Eventually, the fallacy of maturity while they themselves are still young becomes clear. The false perception exposes teens and youth to adult-like situations and opportunities too advanced for them. They no longer want to act their age or be around people of their own age. Sometimes, this results in their becoming sexually active, becoming pregnant, taking drugs, and falling into abusive relationships.

Because of insufficient preventive measures being instilled into the youth in these communities, partly because of absentee parents, kids are left to figure things out on their own, or by experiment.

For some of these young people, having a baby can be a way to fill a void for something they're not getting from their loved ones. Teens and youth may long to have something of their own, or to have someone to care for them in the manner that their child will care for them. They may feel that a child will allow them to escape the negatives going on around them.

They are basically depending on the baby to provide them with happiness and joy, which may give them a sense of hope or purpose.

■ ■ ■

In January of 1994, I met the man who became the father of my son. He was 19 years old, and I was 14.

From the first, I lied to him about my age, telling him I would soon turn 18, and he bought it. I was that mature for my age, or so I thought, and apparently, he was convinced and didn't question it.

I enjoyed his company. Spending time with him was like a breath of fresh air and gave me peace of mind at a time when so much was happening in my life. He came from a grounded family in which his parents were still married and raising their family together. They had already been married 25-plus years when I met him.

Right away we made the most of the time we spent together. Eventually we became sexually intimate and decided to take our relationship more seriously. It was easy for me to let my guard down with him, even though, by this point in my life, I was reserved when it came to letting people into my emotional space.

I managed to mask my emotions, so that I could build a successful relationship minus the drama happening in my life. I didn't want him to experience the chaos, fearing it would run him off. I had to hide the disdain and anger I carried toward my mother. I also tried, upfront, not to be so emotional and needy; I wanted to appear in control and as if I had it all together. Basically, I didn't want my struggles to reflect on the person he was getting involved with.

Prior to meeting him, I was not sexually active; therefore, I was not taking any birth control. In fact, I had never taken contraceptives up to that point, and didn't know much about them. When I had sex before, we had used condoms.

At the time I met my son's father, I was desperate to have someone in my life who didn't cause me pain; someone who could make me smile and fill the void inside me. I wanted someone who could add value to my life and not tear me down; someone who could protect me from hurt; someone who could help me when I couldn't help myself; someone who wouldn't force me to do anything I didn't feel comfortable doing; someone who could guide me in the right direction. He didn't know it, but I needed him long before we met.

His role, by default, would be much bigger than just being my boyfriend. Unbeknownst to him, he would be my peacemaker, my male figure and role model, my security, and more. I hoped he was up for the challenge and wouldn't bail after seeing what was going on in my life, or after he learned what had taken place before his time.

Our first couple of months together were great. When we weren't together, I anxiously looked forward to the next time we would meet. He was fun and became someone I trusted and confided in. As a result of him being an outlet of peace and serenity, my sexual experience with him was different from my first.

Technically, he wasn't my first, but, mentally, he was. This was the first time I felt I had control over something, and was making decisions under normal circumstances (at least what was normal for me). I wasn't forced into doing something I didn't want to do; I didn't feel pressured or uneasy. It didn't hurt or scare me, and I didn't feel obligated, or feel that I was being taken advantage of. Ours was a consensual and mutual decision.

A few months after our sexual encounter, I turned 15 and he thought I was turning 18. In fact, he bought me Happy 18th Birthday cards and balloons. My mother didn't know, at the time, that he was 19, nor did she know I had lied about my age.

Shortly after my 15th birthday, we learned that I was pregnant. He was ecstatic and I was terrified. I wasn't ready for a baby, and I definitely was not ready to tell my mother that I was pregnant at 15; well, technically, it happened at 14, but I didn't find out until after my 15th birthday.

When I could no longer disguise it, I told my mother and she was livid! She also learned then that he was 19 years old. That sent her into even more of a rage, and she was ready to take legal action against him. To keep him from going to jail, I confessed to her that I had lied.

She was upset about everything for months. She tried to persuade me to have an abortion, but I told her that was out of the question.

Having something grow inside me that filled my heart with so much joy made me want this baby even more. I needed this baby. I hadn't planned to get pregnant. I hadn't thought of having a child so early in my life, or in my relationship. It happened because I was negligent. I neglected to use some form of birth control and had unprotected sex.

I realized what I had done was wrong, but I was not going to abort the one opportunity to bring true happiness to my life. I could not abandon this baby like my parents had abandoned me throughout my life.

I knew that having this baby meant I had to prove everyone wrong who had doubted my ability to uphold my responsibilities. I promised myself that even *this* wouldn't stop me from building a brighter future for myself. I would just have to work twice as hard as before.

Eventually, as my pregnancy progressed, my mother became more accepting that I was going ahead with having my baby. Her biggest concern was that I was too young and that she wanted me to have a better chance at a successful future.

At some point, she must have recognized how determined I was and that I wasn't going to let having a baby derail me from my dreams, because she lightened up a bit. My dreams were to be successful in life, and to have a college education and a thriving career at a young age.

From early on, I was always driven and ambitious. It's one of the things my mother admired about me. I recall one day when I had been out taking care of business (opening a bank account, scheduling doctor appointments, and getting information about feeding options). As I got closer to home, I saw my mother standing in the doorway looking at me as I drew closer. She had a look of hope in her eyes, like she was having a proud moment. I believe, when she saw me walking confidently, she realized that I would be okay, and that, for once, since this all started, she had peace of mind. It meant the world to me, knowing that my mother had faith in me.

Although I wasn't legally old enough to work full-time and receive benefits, I did work a youth summer job to generate some income. My son's father had a pretty good job working construction with his dad, so he made up for what I didn't have. He was very responsible and supportive throughout my pregnancy. He gave me money each payday to put into my bank account. We lived in separate homes, but each house was equipped with baby supplies in anticipation of the baby's arrival.

I went into labor a week early, on the night of my boyfriend's birthday. I guess all the dancing and excitement from the party sent me into labor earlier than expected.

We were in bed after the party and I felt my water break. I woke him up, and off to the hospital we went. I was in intense labor for 36 hours before I gave birth to the love of my life on November 21, 1994.

Both of our families came to the hospital while I was in labor.

My mother and sister were present, eagerly awaiting the arrival of their grandson and nephew.

It was a happy time for us all. I was really happy and thankful to have my mother there from beginning to end, walking me through the process. I felt like this was a defining moment in our relationship, and it bonded us on a different level. I was grateful for her support and love during this time, and I don't think it would have been as easy for me if she hadn't been there with me.

After all we had gone through, the hurt and disappointment she had caused me, I still needed her love and support. I needed my mother and she was there for me, as I became a mother to someone who would need me the same way I needed her. It was nice to know that, despite what we had been through, she felt the natural need to be there for me as a new mother, because of how much she loved me. This made my labor much more tolerable, and I was able to get through it with her by my side.

After 36 long hours of pain and no sleep, he finally came. Seeing my son for the first time instantly brought a sense of peace and calmness to my soul. At that moment, he took my mind off of all of the things I had been through up to that very moment. This was the best day ever for me.

After we came home from the hospital, things were a bit better in the first few weeks. It was all about baby James. He put joy in everyone's heart, and, for once, we were functioning like a normal household. My sister was so attached to her nephew that he basically became like one of her stuffed animals that she played with 24/7. It was cute.

My son went to high school with me each day. Adolescent parenting was becoming so common in the urban communities that some inner city high schools opened in-house childcare programs to increase the chances that mothers would graduate high school. My school, North High, just happened to be such a school.

Sometimes, I had to catch the city bus to get to school, so I bought a coat big enough to put him inside in a baby carrier strapped around my shoulders and waist. It looked like I was pregnant with twins when we were all bundled up. We walked about a mile to reach the bus stop, and I carried a diaper bag along with my schoolbag. Sometimes, it was 15 to 20 degrees below zero with snow up to my knees, but we never let that stop us.

Most of the people riding the bus that early in the morning were career professionals commuting to work from their homes in the suburbs. With peculiar looks on their faces, they'd watch me, as if singling me out and judging me.

Some may have assumed I was just another adolescent mother from the urban community with a baby they were paying taxes for. Statistically, I was. What they didn't know was that I wasn't sitting at home collecting a monthly check from the government. I worked just as hard as they did, and I had plans to go to college after high school. After a while, their looks didn't bother me. In time, I would beat the odds of the stereotype and be like them, or *even better*.

Theoretically, I was already winning. I could have taken the easy way out like others had, and gone to an alternative school for young parents for the sake of convenience, and be picked up and dropped off. But I didn't choose to do that. I was not going to allow the state or anyone else to box me in and write me off. Nor was I going to sacrifice or limit my education just because I had a child. I attended a regular high school and received all my credits in preparation for a post-high school education.

While in high school, my mother helped me get a job where she worked. She was a nursing assistant at an elderly home in St. Louis Park, Minnesota. I worked part-time in the kitchen as a dietary aide. I was too young for a full-time job, plus I was still in high school, so I could only work limited hours. On weekends, holidays, and in the summer, I often worked double shifts for extra pay.

During a normal week, my days were filled with school during the day and work in the evenings. Before I had a car, my son's father would get off work, pick us up from school, drop me off at work, and come back to get me when my shift was over. This was our routine. He eventually helped me buy a car, and I could drive myself to and from work.

My days were long and they were tough. Sometimes, I fell asleep on the freeway while driving to work. I was exhausted and not getting enough rest between caring for my son, completing my homework, and working.

I really had no idea what I signed up for when I became pregnant. Life as I knew it, as a carefree teenager, was gone. I was now a robot! I knew I had to work to survive and provide for my son, regardless of how much his father contributed. I was not going to be solely dependent on him and have to ask for handouts.

I was now embarking on a journey of perseverance for long-term success. I couldn't give up or look back, because no one else would have my back. The more I understood that, the more I pushed myself to work harder each day.

Most of my life, I had wanted to be a teacher, but when I became a mother, I had to put that dream on the back burner, in favor of a more lucrative profession. I had to pick a field that was competitive and that paid very well.

While I was in high school, the childcare program director,

Gwen, and her colleague, Kirsten, invited working professionals to speak to us about career choices after graduation.

One speaker in particular caught my attention, talking about computers and Information Technology (IT). Gwen arranged for us to go on an informational visit to the office of the computer professionals; at that point, I realized I was leaning toward a career in IT. Not only was it highly competitive and paid very well, it was also intriguing. Needless to say, it was the field I would major in after high school. Until then, I focused on finishing high school.

In my mind and in the minds of so many other youth, I thought I was mature for my age because of my experiences growing up. I thought I was mature enough to take on the huge responsibility of motherhood. However, I hadn't thought through the logistics, such as being old enough to legally work full-time hours and receive health benefits. I hadn't thought about being of legal age to sign documents on behalf of my child, or about how to become financially stable to raise my son.

I didn't realize I had so much life left to live as a child, which didn't coincide with being a mother. I was simply a child making adult decisions from a child's point-of-view, which is why it was tougher than if I had been an adult.

Too often, we experience situations we feel shape us into something we are not. Just because I'd had to use my best judgment and think like an adult, didn't mean I was ready for the actual adult role of having a child. Those experiences just made me wiser and stronger, but *did not make me grow up any faster*.

I didn't realize until it was too late that I had put the cart before the horse. If it weren't for my son's father, I would not have made enough money to support my son and me. I wasn't even old enough to make legal decisions for his health and other things. Based on the laws of the country, I wasn't mature enough to raise a child, because I was still a child myself. I was a dependent, responsible for raising another dependent. I had to do the best I could until I came of legal age to start the next chapter in my life—going to college and landing a full-time job with benefits.

Raising a child could have been a much better experience had I waited longer to become a mom. I would have been better able to enjoy the beauty of motherhood, rather than the daily struggles. It was hard enough getting through such a dysfunctional upbringing; adding a baby to the mix made it twice as hard. Nevertheless, I had to live up to my responsibilities. It wasn't impossible; it just meant I had to work much harder at it.

Like so many youth today, I was looking for love for all the wrong reasons. I was too young to long for a husband, but I was young enough to long for a father, security, stability, and the love of a parent. I thought being with my son's father would close those gaps, or satisfy the feeling of being cared for. What I hadn't realized was, I didn't get to know him for who he was to see if I would have fallen in love with that person. Instead, I got what I needed from him and became complacent.

Unfortunately, this happens more than we realize or want to admit. Young women and men get involved in relationships looking for something they didn't get while growing up. In looking for happiness or looking to fill a void, some may jump from one relationship to another.

Before getting serious, I should have resolved some of the personal issues I had that might have affected future relationships. Had I been at peace with myself, I perhaps could have better developed a real friendship with my son's father—before getting serious.

I should have been looking for the qualities I like most in a companion, and not the qualities I wished my parents had had.

However, at the age of 14, I hadn't lived long enough to know what those qualities were. I still had a lot of living to do to make that determination. I had some idea, of course, based on the traditional values and morals that I grew up with, but I was too inexperienced to know what I wanted in a long-term relationship.

If I could do it over, I would have casually dated first. That way, I could have focused on building a better me, despite my upbringing or shortcomings.

Besides searching for love in relationships, I believed that having a child would fill the same void. When I became pregnant, my thinking was more emotional than logical. I had hoped this baby would bring me joy and happiness, despite the challenges at home. I was overcome with the anticipation of the love and affection this baby would bring, instead of the reality of my poor choice and its impact on my baby's life and mine. To me, this baby was the way to experience the love and bond of a mother and her child. I wished for a stronger and more loving bond with my mother, and now I could personally experience what that felt like.

Though I was creating a strong bond with my own child, I never stopped needing my mother. Despite what we had gone through, I needed her in that delivery room with me. I was terrified, and the only person who could help make me feel safe was my mother. I felt like a little girl all over again, wanting my mother by my side. Her being there made me feel like I did matter, and that I was still her little girl. It meant the world to me and showed me that I still needed my mommy, just like my son needed me.

I was determined *not* to live up to or bring any truth to the stereotype of being an adolescent mother. In fact, that stereotype motivated me to push myself harder each day toward building a brighter future, partly because society had already decided I would be a failure.

According to the U.S. Census Bureau, Current Population Survey 2012 (*http://www.familyfacts.org/briefs/35/family-structure-and-childrens-education*), single-mother households make up half of all households in poverty (51.5 percent). This same study shows that one in two children living in unmarried, single-mother households are poor. The poverty rate for children in female householder families is 58.1 percent in the U.S.

These stereotypes can and do impede adolescent parents, because society has already singled them out and *expects* them to amount to nothing, so they comply and give up hope without even trying. Discouraged, they're deterred from pursuing their dreams, or thinking bigger. They become what society has painted them to be.

It can happen to anyone, especially young people, if they have no one in their corner to encourage them; someone to inspire and mentor them; to provide positive influence and guidance on thinking past just being an adolescent parent. Encouragement and reinforcement make a difference and give them hope that they can still succeed.

Fortunately for me, someone intervened with this needed encouragement. Their affirmation assured me that I didn't have to give up on my dreams because I became a parent too early. It just meant I had to work more aggressively to achieve my goals. Riding public transportation to school in the morning helped fuel my ambitions to be successful in life and prove society wrong.

Even though some of the professionals riding the bus may have judged me, I wanted my accomplishments to prove them wrong. I wanted to show other adolescent parents that they don't have to cave in to societal perceptions. If they try hard, they can still do what others do, maybe even better.

Statistics also show, according to the same U.S. Census Bureau survey, that non-poor families with a female householder are 15.2 percent of all non-poor families in the U.S. These were the statistics of which I was determined to *not* become a part.

I could beat the odds and exceed stereotypical expectations early on, because I was determined to not allow my mistakes and poor choices defeat me. I turned those experiences into *opportunities and motivational tactics* to do better. It wasn't rocket science; all it took was faith in God and myself, willpower and determination. I had a vision for my life. I set attainable goals, and I executed a strategy and plan to achieve them, one by one.

Being a teen mom, I knew I had very little room for mistakes, so I took advantage of every opportunity that came my way. Attending the career fair at school gave me insight into professional careers, post-high school. I took this opportunity seriously and looked further into the career choices that interested me most, since I didn't have a lot of time between high school graduation day and college registration day.

After the informational interview, I had a better understanding of my first choice in professional careers, so that I could speak with my high school and college counselors about it. This was one of the times where I had made a conscious effort to think maturely about my options and the opportunities that would follow. A year prior, I would have overlooked the potential this career fair offered, but becoming a mother made me think differently.

I realized I could no longer overlook or pass up life-changing opportunities, and that I had to act on them as they presented themselves.

The career fair was one of those life-changing opportunities, and I'm thankful I maximized every bit of it. By taking it seriously and looking into it further, I had done the best thing for my son and myself.

Key Takeaway from Chapter Seven

Ready too soon.

More Takeaways...

- Making sure that my son had a father present in his life made a significant impact on my son's life and mine.

- My son's father was willingly involved with caregiving and helped me support my son financially, a true blessing because I was not legally of age to work enough hours to support us.

- Establishing independence was important because it was possible that no one else would have my back. Understanding that made me push myself to work harder each day.

- To ensure our future, I had to pick a field that was competitive and highly compensated.

- My struggles and hardships were motivational tactics I used to find better opportunities.

- As a teenage parent, I had very little room for mistakes, so I took advantage of every opportunity as it presented itself.

- The career fair at school provided insight into a variety of post-high school professional careers.

- Being judged for being a young mother motivated me to prove the naysayers wrong and accomplish the unexpected.

- I wanted to show other adolescent parents that they don't have to give in to society's perceptions, or be boxed in and limit their potential.

- My mother's faith in me—that I would succeed regardless of my current situation—meant the world to me.

- I was determined to not allow mistakes or poor choices defeat me, and, early on, I beat the odds and surpassed stereotypical expectations.

EIGHT

Him

Having a child so young was a great challenge for me. I was now responsible for effectively managing someone else's life, having failed to manage my own. The good thing was, I could teach him what I had learned from my mistakes and poor choices.

My life as a new mother changed my thinking—I was now making choices for two of us—and I had to make a lot more sacrifices than I had ever imagined myself making. Adolescent life no longer looked the same.

The initial adjustment to motherhood was huge and seemed like it would never normalize. I had to adjust to the new operating rhythm I had adopted. His needs now came before mine. The things I had done just for me were history. I was living for this beautiful baby boy who had captivated my heart.

Over the years, we grew close, since we were close in age, giving us a unique and versatile relationship. There were times when I was the strict, traditional mother, and there were times when I was the cool and adaptable mother who could relate to his era.

We shared a lot in common, which made it easier for us to get along and understand one another. Some of the same fads that were popular for my age group were also popular for his—for the most part. It was a gift and a curse, because many of the negative things going on within my generation were also problems within his. This made me twice as leery about how he grew up and the choices he made.

Despite the stereotype I lived with as an adolescent parent, this experience was more of a motivation than a hindrance for me. My dream of a brighter, more successful future was now urgent. Life had to speed up so that I could create stability and security for us. I couldn't take my time deciding what I wanted to be when I grew up and what route to take. I had to maximize the value of current opportunities, all the while using my actions as a learning experience for my son, so that he understood that actions and results can be positive or negative.

As things got better for us, I never felt a need to overcompensate for the things I didn't have growing up. Whatever I felt in my heart to give to my son, I gave him. My goal now was to teach him the importance of good work ethics and the essentials of hard work.

I wanted to convey to him that most things in life don't come easily, and that he would have to work hard to be successful. My way of demonstrating this message was through my actions. I also made it a point to explain that, along the way, I hoped he'd benefit from what I had done and would see what success looks like.

Although I shielded him as best I could from knowing about our hardships, I instilled values that would position him to be successful and modest throughout his life's journey. Values that would help him appreciate the blessings given to him to get an education and to be in control of his destiny; values that would teach him to learn from missed opportunities, mistakes, and poor choices, as well as the importance of helping and giving back to others.

I may have let him off easy, at times, perhaps spoiling him a bit, but, for the most part, he had to earn his keep. I didn't want him growing up with the misconception that things would be handed to him, or that he should depend on others to get ahead. I wanted him to be as self-sufficient as possible, so that he understood that *failure is not an option.*

In addition to teaching him traditional American morals and values, I made sure he had a sense of religion and a Christian belief system. He was raised going to church and has a great relationship with God. He's not perfect, but he is far from being a troubled kid. Thus far, most of the feedback I've gotten from random people regarding my son has been consistently about his kindness and the good manners he displays to others.

But, when it comes to school, the feedback is the complete opposite. His teachers usually love and adore him, but, boy, was he a chatterbox in class; a social butterfly who couldn't wait to see his friends at school. That's how it was through 12th grade.

I was ecstatic when he graduated high school and started college. I no longer received letters and phone calls from school about too much socializing during class.

One of the most profound things about being a mother to my son is letting him know, on a regular basis, how much I love him. I tend to overcompensate with my displays of affection. I've always kissed, hugged, and held him more than the norm, even when he became an adult. I make sure to tell him that I love him just about every time we speak. It feels natural for me.

I love loving my son and I don't think that will ever lessen. I wouldn't solely attribute it to my lack of affection from my parents as a child, but more because it's a genuine, natural feeling to give that amount of love to him every day. Even at the tender age of 20, he knows I need to get my daily dose of hugs and kisses.

I never understood how it wasn't a natural instinct in all mothers to show their children love and affection. It's always perplexed me why my mother didn't show me this type of love, considering it isn't something that has to be taught. It wasn't taught to me; it was natural from the first time I held my son in my arms. Regardless of the reason, my son will always know that I love him, even when it's tough love that he needs, at times.

It wasn't always easy, tough love. It hurt me more than it hurt him, but I'd rather he learns the consequences of his actions from me, than from someone else later. I can't prevent life from happening to him, but I can, at least, prepare him for how to deal with it.

One of the things I appreciated about my mother was that she gave it to us, raw and uncut. She didn't hold back any punches, and because of that, neither do I. I don't sugarcoat anything when it comes to teaching him right from wrong, as I know it to be. He may think I'm heartless at those times, but if I don't tell him straight up, then jail, violence, drugs, depression, or death will.

I may not be able to prevent the not-so-good choices he makes, but at least he will have a realistic understanding of what will happen because of those decisions. If he chooses to go through with it—and I imagine he will, from time to time—then I must also let him learn from it and not jump to his rescue (which is easier said than done, by the way). It's the best way and how I learned; therefore, I'm confident he'll be okay. Besides, he has some of me in him, so I know he will be resilient and undefeated in life.

I feel that I've laid the right foundation for him to build on, and I have no doubt that he will do just that. He'll undoubtedly face obstacles along the way, but, with faith and determination, he'll be successful.

Instilling meaningful morals and values in children is the parents' responsibility, regardless of how young or old the children are. Even though I was just a child myself when I gave birth to my son, my obligation wasn't at all lessened. Living these meaningful morals and values, providing these tools, can help him prevent making the same mistakes I did at his age. These values and lessons can increase his chances of becoming a Good Samaritan, an advocate for others, a success, and wiser as he grows into adulthood.

I did not want him to become a parent too young, as I had, so I made sure he had opportunities that prevented that from happening. He kept busy with sports, he was involved with our church's youth group, and I made sure he kept up with school.

My job has been to give him a fair chance at life and to ensure he had opportunities that would afford him a successful future. With that said, I thought I had to be tough on him and create stricter boundaries for him.

I was passionate about helping him understand the importance of getting it right the *first* time. I talked with him about how it takes only one slip or one poor decision to ruin his life, or get him into a heap of trouble. I did this because I was fearful he might follow in others' footsteps, people who were not making good choices.

I did all I could to prevent him from becoming a follower, from joining gangs, doing drugs, from losing motivation, and developing low self-esteem. Hopefully one day he'll understand that his best interests were my number one priority, and that I felt it was my duty to show him the way—even if it meant being tough on him at times.

Key Takeaway from Chapter Eight

It was all up to me.

More Takeaways...

- My life changed as a new mother, because I was no longer deciding for just myself.

- I was now responsible for managing someone else's life better and more effectively than I had managed my own.

- I had little time to decide what route to take when I grew up.

- The dream of living a bright and successful future was now urgent.

- I took advantage of opportunities as they presented themselves, and maximized their value for our future.

- I took seriously my motherly duties of showing my son the importance of good work ethics and the essentials of hard work.

- I took seriously my most important motherly duty to put religion into my son's life.

- I wanted my son to be as self-sufficient as possible, so that he would know and understand that *failure is not an option.*

NINE

The Root of My Problems, and Their Solutions

Moving to Minnesota was probably my mother's best attempt to get help for overcoming her addictions. Minnesota offered her services and resources that weren't available in Gary, Indiana.

It was the first time someone *outside* of our household even noticed that something was wrong *inside* our household. Being taken from home the first time was the start of a long road to redemption. My mother was ordered by the court to get into professional treatment each time she relapsed. We were placed in temporary living arrangements while she got better. It became a cycle.

My mother's fight to remain sober and clean was very challenging for her. She did well for short periods of time, but would break under pressure, or succumb to temptations. Some of her relapses began with marijuana, and she gradually made her way back to smoking crack. When I realized she was smoking marijuana while trying to remain sober, I would be greatly concerned.

I pleaded with her to stop smoking marijuana, fearing it would lead to the other drugs. She would assure me it wouldn't, but I wasn't convinced. It was just a matter of time before she was using crack again, and the thought of it terrified me. One high led to another, and before I knew it, she was repeating the old drug addiction patterns and behavior.

While I was working at the nursing home in high school, the relationship between my mother and me was pretty rocky. We clashed a lot, mainly due to her drug use and its ramifications on our family. She continued making the same poor choices that had led to our tumultuous past.

I had had enough. I was no longer going to allow her to exempt herself from her actions. It wasn't only about me, but also how it was impacting my sister.

My disdain and frustration toward my mother strained our relationship. I'd become very resentful, mainly when she got high.

At times, she came to work high, barely able to function. She looked really bad. Those times at work were mentally and emotionally tough for me. Sometimes, I'd start crying. It was extremely painful to see my mother like this, looking like she was going through a rough time.

A lot of times, she hadn't eaten properly, mainly because she didn't have the money to buy lunch. On days like this, I'd fix a plate for her and set it aside, so that she'd have something to eat.

I had mixed emotions. I'd suddenly become angry and frustrated seeing her in the condition she was in. It wasn't fair that those problems followed me to work—the one place where I thought I could escape them. I needed to be able to focus on my job and keep a clear mind. I shouldn't have to stress out in the dumping room about my mother's current state of well-being, and worry about my sister.

My mother constantly put pressure and stress on me.

One day, one of the registered nurses came into the kitchen, looking for me. She looked concerned, as she asked me to follow her to the basement. She pushed the bathroom door open and there was my mother, lying on the floor, barely coherent.

We got her to her feet. The nurse knew my mother had a drug problem, and this was not the first time she had found her like this. In fact, it wasn't my first time, either. However, on that day, she wasn't as out of it as she had been the last time.

The nurse was a very caring woman and she had patiently tried to work with my mother to get her help; but this time, that was it.

She had to follow protocol and report it, and I didn't blame her. It was not okay to put residents and staff members' lives at risk because a co-worker was under the influence of drugs. The residents' lives had been entrusted to her, and I know from experience the type of harm her condition could cause for others.

I became angry, seeing my mother stretched out on the bathroom floor in this state. Hell, I was enraged! Did she not think about how this mentally and emotionally affected me? Did she even care about how it hurt me to see her like this? Problem is, she didn't, and for this, I was pissed! I had enough vile memories of similar situations that I have yet to rid from my memory. Seeing her now, disheveled and completely out of it, made me distraught and incapable of continuing to work. I was sad and depressed and worried about her the rest of the day.

These events caused dark days for me. No matter how much time had passed, I never got used to it, and I could never accept my mother under these circumstances. Each time hurt me just as much as it had the first time.

Over time, I became fed up with my mother's drug use and her irresponsibility. I was tired of her thinking only of herself and not considering how this was affecting us. I was no longer going to excuse her selfish, irresponsible behavior, to dismiss what had happened once she became coherent again. I was no longer going to allow her to get off easy.

Whenever I noticed she was high, I talked to her with disgust and disapproval of her choices. I talked to her as if I was the adult and she was the child. I'm not sure how much of what I said sunk in, because all I got was a blank look, her brain too numb or too slow to process what I was saying. Had she been sober, she would have knocked my teeth down my throat, literally, because she didn't tolerate any disrespect or back-talk from us (no pun intended).

I was becoming bitter and angry with her. I was tired of having to be the adult in our family, having to play her role *and* mine;

constantly begging her not to use, and encouraging her to make the right choices, for her sake and ours. If she didn't want to be a mother, then she shouldn't have signed up for it. *She* was supposed to be the one giving sound advice and showing concern about *my* well-being. It was her duty as a mother, and she wasn't fulfilling it. I didn't have time to make many mistakes or enjoy my childhood like I could and should have, because I was too busy babysitting her and raising my sister.

The reason her behavior bothered me so much was because she was still doing what she had done to cause us to grow up the way we did. She was still using the same substances that prevented her from protecting me from the creeps who took advantage of me, physically and sexually; the substance that drove me to someone twice my age for the comfort and support she should have given me; the substance that prevented her from helping me overcome my fears by teaching me how to fight back and say no; the substance that allowed me to feel that isolation and disconnection from society was normal. After all this time, things just were not getting any better.

Enough was enough. When was she going to get it? When was she going to want better for herself? Better yet, when was she going to fight for her three children? I couldn't understand why she couldn't stop or make it go away. I often wondered why it was so difficult for her to choose us over the drugs.

I had reached my breaking point. I could no longer allow her addiction, nor my time and energy spent helping her fight it to consume my life. It finally occurred to me that she didn't want to fight it or stop it. I was deteriorating on a daily basis, at times becoming dark and depressed. I wanted to be free, and I knew I had to make drastic changes to be free.

Living with a parent or loved one who is battling drug or substance abuse isn't easy. Life can feel dark and grim. At some point, we have to muster up enough strength to know when to let go or walk away. It doesn't mean we don't love our loved ones, or that we're turning our backs on them. It's mainly so we can accept what we cannot change, and to prevent their behavior from having a negative effect on our lives. Quite often, people get lost amidst their loved ones' poor choices or issues, and end up suffering from it.

Some of us feel compelled to help or take on our loved ones' problems, at any cost, out of guilt or obligation. People like me feel it's our duty. What we fail to realize—and I certainly did most of my life—is that we are all individuals responsible for making our own choices and decisions. I wish I'd had the strength to draw a line in the sand, or set boundaries earlier on regarding how far and how deeply I would allow my mother's choices to affect me. I wish I hadn't allowed them to push me to a breaking point that affected me mentally, emotionally, and physically. By the time I realized I needed to make a change, so much damage had already been done.

I would have saved myself a lot of headaches and disappointment if I knew then what I know now—that my mother had to fight for herself. If she wasn't fighting for herself, she wasn't going to get better, and neither would my own health.

This experience has taught me that I must focus on my responsibilities and myself before I can help others. My son was my priority, and if I was putting my health at risk, I was not being the best I could be for my son. I was robbing him and myself of enjoying the life and advantages of not going down the same path my mother had chosen to go down. Some days felt like I was the one with these issues and addictions, because of my level of involvement while caring for her, showing tough love to her, and raising my sister and myself.

I had to start thinking about my son and myself. I could no longer let my mother's problems bring me down or have such a significant effect on me. I needed to be mentally strong for my son. I also had to be healthy enough to pick up the pieces and provide love and support to my sister in my mother's absences and downfalls. If I continued to let my mother's actions affect me negatively, I could lose sight of my goals and ambitions.

When the light went on, I concluded that I would stop suffering from her actions. I was not going to live my life as if *I* was the one getting high and neglecting my kids and responsibilities. It wasn't fair. I worked hard to not make the same mistakes, so it wasn't fair that she continued to put me through it.

I could have easily become unmotivated, addicted to drugs, sex, or men. Opportunities presented themselves daily, because it was all that was around me. I chose to abstain from that lifestyle, not solely for myself but because I had to think about how it would affect my family.

As a 16-year-old mother and high school student, I knew I had to move out of my mother's home so that I could succeed with my goals.

Key Takeaway from Chapter Nine

Enough.

More Takeaways...

- I finally stopped fighting someone else's addictions. They had consumed my life.

- If my mother didn't fight for herself, she wouldn't get better, and neither would my health if I didn't step back.

- Putting yourself first doesn't mean you don't care, or that you're turning your back; it's merely accepting what you can't change and preventing the negative effect it has on your life.

- My son was my priority and I couldn't be the best I could be for him, if my health was at risk because of my mother's stressful behaviors.

- I needed to be mentally strong for my son, so I could be a good mother, while avoiding repeating my mother's mistakes.

- It was incumbent on me to avoid choices and situations that would cause my family to suffer.

TEN

Living Together as Parents

I moved in with my son's father and his family when I was 16 years old. Things just weren't getting better at home, and I didn't want to raise my son in such a hostile and toxic environment. My mother couldn't keep her bills paid, and she constantly violated the terms and conditions of her probation. My sister went back into foster care, and my brother was out on his own.

At this time, I was considered emancipated and able to live on my own without having to go into the state's care.

Being away from my sister again was very hard. I wished I could have gotten custody of her and never have to worry about her leaving me again, but the state didn't consider me old enough. I took advantage of every opportunity to be with her, though, while she was in the foster home. I wanted to protect her and be there with her every night as she went to sleep, and every morning when she awakened. I loved my sister as if I had given birth to her, and I felt it was my big-sister duty to protect her. Unfortunately, that decision was out of my control and I had to accept whatever time with her that I could get.

Fortunately for us, the foster home my sister lived in at the time allowed her to visit me on weekends. It was nice that my son's father and his family let her come and stay with us when the foster home permitted. They knew how much it meant to me, and they were very supportive, considering all that my family was going through. Whenever I had my sister, I felt I had to be mother, brother, and stepfather, so that she had that sense of completeness. I tried filling any void by spending quality time with her when she visited.

On one occasion, we had gone to the supermarket with my son's grandmother. As we headed toward our car with the groceries, my son's grandmother turned and asked me, "Ki-Ki (which is my nickname), isn't that your mother?" and she pointed to a parked car. I looked and it was, indeed, my mom. She was with the guy she had been seeing for a while. I guess you could say he was her boyfriend. She looked like she had been out all night partying, judging by her appearance and the clothes she was wearing.

She tried to slouch down so that I couldn't see her, but it was too late. As soon as my son's grandmother pointed her out, I looked directly at my mother. It didn't matter how far down she slid, I knew it was her.

I became extremely emotional at seeing her, and at our current situation. If my sister had seen her, she would have broken her neck to get to my mother, so I immediately distracted her from seeing mommy or figuring out what was going on.

At that moment, my mother was in no position to be a mother to us, and I didn't want my sister or myself to get hurt any more than we already were. I could not bear my sister being overcome with sorrow because she couldn't be with our mother.

This event took me back to the time in Gary, Indiana, when she left us all day without any food and had the nerve to drive past our house, sliding down in her seat. It was déjà vu, because I was the one who had spotted her then.

Our mother didn't get out of the car, or even acknowledge us as we faced each other. They hurried away, and so did we.

I could tell that my son's grandmother knew I was really hurt by what had just happened. My mom looked a mess, and here my sister and I were, living with other people because of what I just saw in that car. She chose that life over us, and it hurt.

For the most part, my son's father and his family were very supportive of me, and made me feel like I was a part of the family. There were some who weren't as supportive, however, and that made it quite challenging for me to be there.

Later, I realized the problem was beyond me and that they had self-esteem issues of their own, which conflicted with anyone who was ambitious and driven in life. I managed to stay focused and not let anyone's personal issues affect me or get in the way of my goals.

Over the years, I have learned that the bad comes with the good. Unfortunately, not everyone will be happy or supportive of your success, and that's okay. I understand now why it's extremely important to be deeply rooted and grounded so that you're not easily derailed by others' malicious or harmful intents. It's also extremely important to be aware and to recognize when this happens.

If anything, that experience made me wiser and less naïve in thinking that everyone has good intentions. I learned to stay true to myself and to focus on my goals without seeking approval from others.

Despite one person's negativity, there were good times with the family. They were a tight-knit family, and they spent a lot of time together. They loved to gather in the kitchen and play games, cook, and have fun. This was their normal routine, and I appreciated it for my son's sake, because I couldn't give him that. I would get in on the fun at times, but, most of the time, I stayed to myself in our upstairs bedroom. This was primarily to avoid confrontation, but also because I was more comfortable being with myself.

As time passed, my son's father and I weren't seeing eye-to-eye. Our days as a couple were numbered, as I kept up with school and work. We continued our union as parents to our son, but that was the extent of it.

After I finished high school, I moved out, intending to get a place of my own. I temporarily moved in with my mother until I could find someplace for myself.

Although my relationship with my son's father fell apart early, we remained friends so that we could effectively co-parent our son. He was still a great father and financial provider for our son, although we lived in separate households. Our joint parenting made it easier for me to pursue college and work full-time.

Considering all that was going on at home—being a mother, student, and working—it later occurred to me that it was not the best time to pursue a relationship. I had too many things going on that required my full attention. I couldn't give my all to a relationship, simply because I was stretched too thin already.

Some of the stress and pressure that had caused us to grow apart eased, after deciding to end my relationship with my son's father. I had taken on too much, and I didn't want any relationship to slow me down or cause me to fail. I didn't want to rob myself of having a fair chance at happiness and bliss, so choosing to end it was one of the best decisions I could have made for both our sakes. I became a better mother and student, and I worked even harder at school and at my full-time job.

Sometimes we have to make sacrifices and tough decisions we may not like, but in the long run, they're the best decisions for our loved ones and for ourselves. I had become complacent during my stay with my son's father, and having support every day. It had taken a load off my shoulders when it came to our son. However, I had to look at the bigger picture and do what I felt was necessary to maintain a healthy relationship for us as parents, to create my own identity, and to establish independence.

In the end, stepping out on my own only helped to make me stronger as a woman and mother.

Key Takeaway from Chapter Ten

Choose what's best over what's preferred.

More Takeaways...

- Choosing what is best is rewarding, but requires continuous practice and sacrifice.

- As I grew in my responsibilities, my priorities shifted.

- I often made decisions I didn't like, but knew they were best for me and my future.

- To consider the impact for the short-term and long-term, I adjusted my thinking to look at the bigger picture.

- Finding love and long-term relationships took a lower priority so I could focus on being the best mother I could be, while finishing college and building a career.

- To establish independence and maintain a healthy relationship with my son's father, it was better for me to end our relationship.

- The best decisions can be the most painful decisions, but they often render the best results.

ELEVEN

Challenges of Being Independent

Life is quite different when you first step out on your own. Taking on bills and expenses by yourself can take some getting used to. You no longer have reinforcement from your parents, or the support you had when you were someone else's dependent. You either sink or you swim, depending on what you do and how disciplined you are.

While I was a teenager, I looked forward to getting my own place and being free and independent. I imagined it would be easy and lots of fun. I hadn't imagined the hardships or struggles involved, nor did I fully understand why I needed to change the way I lived at the time. It didn't dawn on me that I had to revamp my entire way of thinking. I could no longer make the same choices, or do the same things I'd done when I had more support.

The reality was that life was no longer the same, and successfully meeting my new challenges required that I start thinking like a responsible adult ASAP. My entire mindset regarding my friends and associates had to change.

Changes were also necessary regarding how I managed my paycheck—saving more of it and living within the budget I developed. I also had to become more business-minded to properly handle my affairs. Life as I knew it totally changed.

I got my first two-bedroom apartment when I was 19. My mother's drug use continued, affecting my sister's well-being, so I took custody of her and she came to live with me. She was finally where she belonged. From that day forward, I vowed to protect her.

She and my son lived like siblings—and fought like them, as well. They drove me crazy! Although the two of them were a handful, they were the wind beneath my wings. They were daily reminders why I had to keep pushing. As overwhelming as it could sometimes be, *failure was not an option.*

I had a steady job and reliable transportation, but I was far from where I wanted to be in life. There were obstacles I overcame, and obstacles I accepted.

In the beginning, I struggled financially for what seemed like an eternity. It felt like I would never come out of the storm, or see daylight at the end of the tunnel.

Asking for help never came easily for me, mostly because there was no one for me to ask. More importantly, I had disciplined myself throughout my life to work hard at getting what I needed or wanted. I've always been considerate in not burdening others by asking for anything. If I couldn't make it happen by myself, then it just wasn't meant to be, or maybe not meant for me to have at the time. I live by this rule to this day and I've taught my son the same.

It was hard juggling our living expenses all at once: my son's, my sister's, and my own. I had to find a balance between necessities and wants. To make ends meet, I worked a full-time and a part-time job while going to school.

As I became financially independent, I made a lot of poor choices, sometimes having my priorities out of order. For instance, I reneged paying major bills to have fun shopping or treat myself. It took a while to develop the habit of paying what was most important first and become financially stable and responsible.

I often went through spells where I became weary and wanted to give up. Finishing college and working in a well-paying career seemed farfetched. During those times, I temporarily lost sight of the bigger picture. I grew tired of struggling and working so hard for something that seemed impossible because it was so far into the future.

What kept me going was knowing I had no one else on earth

who had my back if I lost it all. I had no other option but to keep going and to succeed. I at least owed it to my son, if to no one else.

I was never lost for long. Once reality sunk in again, I would get back on track, pushing myself even harder. During those moments when I felt like letting go, I would remind myself how far I had come and how close I was to the finish line. Looking at my son and knowing he was counting on me was my main source of strength and helped keep me going.

Going through such hardships definitely helped me mature. As I became more responsible, I started making wiser choices.

The hardships also brought me much closer to God. Prayer gave me peace, hope, and resolution. It helped to restore my faith when things reached the point that I was uncertain if they were going to get better. God always made up for my shortcomings; when I was negligent or irresponsible, *He* somehow provided a way for us. *He* was very patient with me, as I finally got the hang of being a responsible adult, creating financial security for my family and me.

I can't attribute all my hardships to my foibles. Some challenges were due to the cost of living as a single parent with a standard income and no college education. Rent, car notes, insurance, utilities, and daycare were almost impossible to keep up with for a person like me. Although I was working full-time, I was barely making ends meet. I had gotten a full-time job right out of high school as a customer service representative for a bank. I was also a full-time student at a local junior college, majoring in Computer Networking and Administration. This was the field I became interested in because of the career fair I attended in high school. At that time, I met with a college counselor to learn more about the IT field, decided to get an Associates in Applied Science (A.A.S) degree, and then transfer to a four-year university.

My goal out of high school was to get a job within a company's IT organization that would afford me the opportunity to excel, and where I could apply my college degree. The bank was that company.

I started in Customer Service while in junior college. My idea was to get my foot in the door, no matter how near the bottom I had to start.

As I got closer to finishing my degree, I began looking for opportunities within the company's IT organization. I found one that fit my major, so I went on an informational interview to get a feel for what it was like.

Once I finished my A.A.S degree, I applied for a job within the Technology Center where they provided help desk support for Local Area Networks (LANs). I helped troubleshoot and resolve issues dealing with company computers, bank applications, accounts, servers, printers, backups, and installations.

Although I was making more money than I had as a customer service rep, it still wasn't enough to make ends meet.

I was now attending a four-year university where I majored in Computer Science. I made the tough decision to pick up a part-time job to keep my head above water. This meant more time away from my son. It often bothered me that I couldn't be there for my baby when he got home from daycare, or prepare his dinner in the evenings. Some nights I couldn't tuck him into bed because I had to work.

Even though I felt bad about not being there for him more, I would have felt worse if I couldn't feed him, put clothes on his back, or provide a roof over his head. This is what assured me I was making the best decision when I doubted myself as a mother. I knew it was only temporary, and that it was extremely important for me to get a college education so that I could work smarter and not harder.

I had to make sure that our financial hardships weren't transparent to my son.

There were times when I could barely afford to give my son lunch money after paying bills and taking care of expenses, and times when I sacrificed buying myself lunch so that I could put gas in my car. Even though my son's father paid child support, it still wasn't enough to cover the cost of living for the two of us.

I was blessed to find a high-paying, part-time job with flexible hours for the city of Minneapolis. For the time being, the job helped to fill in the financial gaps, and I enjoyed working with the people. They became our extended family and like our second home. My son's father would bring him to me around the time I was getting off work, since it was so late. He and I were a team, just not a romantic team.

My son would come in and have a seat while I wrapped things up. He enjoyed coming to mommy's workplace and being around my co-workers. This really helped take away some of the burden of being away from him while I worked. Since he looked forward to being there, that made it all worthwhile.

My son was like a soldier who helped to keep mommy grounded in the battle to succeed. He didn't complain about much, unless he wanted the new Power Rangers toy that just came out! Other than that, he was mommy's "rider." He went with the flow and adjusted easily to our circumstances.

After I got acclimated in my help desk support role while pursuing my degree in Computer Science, I started searching for my next career move in the IT division. Here I could use my current skills and learn more about IT as it pertained to data, analysis, software development, relational databases, security, infrastructure, and architecture.

I found an opportunity in the Enterprise Data Warehouse and applied for the job. I was hired and, once again, I started at the bottom. The job paid more money, and I was on my way to building my future.

I started out as a production operator. In this capacity, I learned about the business, systems, and applications supported. I also learned to program in various software languages. Fortunately, I had learned the fundamentals of most of these languages in my studies. That gave me leverage, and it wasn't long before I was well on my way. I took a lot of training and I did a lot of self-teaching, studying manuals, user guides, and Computer-Based Training (CBT) courses.

Once I had the basics down, I could use what I had learned and build on it in my own sandbox. Eventually, that led to me becoming a software developer, which opened the door for more opportunities and growth.

In addition to my own growing success, my sister was doing well in high school, allowing her to complete her studies six months early. After the winter break of her senior year, she didn't have to return until June for graduation, since she had earned all her high school credits. By then, her post-secondary schooling was underway, as she pursued a career in Cosmetology at Aveda Institute.

As my career advanced, so did my salary. I was now making enough money to live comfortably.

We had lived in my first and only apartment for six years, when I decided it was time to buy a house. Although we had created fun memories in our two-bedroom apartment, I was ready to give my son and myself more. I wanted him to experience home ownership, and to show him that hard work does pay off. I bought a beautiful house in a prestigious neighborhood in the North Minneapolis-Camden area. At age 25, I was living among other homeowners who were much older than I was. We were one of the few African American families either living in that community, or owning a home there.

Establishing independence isn't always easy. For me and for many others, it's extremely difficult, and comes with lots of challenges to manage. Eventually, however, I got the hang of it. I wished I would have known what to expect, so that I could have been better prepared. When I had someone else to lean on, I developed certain patterns of behavior that no longer fit with my life.

I quickly learned that living on your own takes discipline and sacrifice. I now had a bigger purpose in life and had to make wiser decisions. The things I did when I had fewer responsibilities no longer worked. I had to plan, budget, and develop business acumen to properly manage my affairs.

Moving out on my own actually shaped me into a better person and forced me to mature. It took time and trial and error, but I eventually got the swing of things and was motivated to keep excelling. What I was working toward was much bigger than the *immediate gratification* I would have gotten from those things for which I thought I was willing to compromise.

The advice I would offer to anyone growing into the position of responsible adulthood is to keep an open mind. There will be times when you have to pick your battles and choose the ones that offer a bigger gain. In other words, you will have to see the bigger picture and distinguish between the necessities and the *wants*, and then make sacrifices accordingly.

Making the wrong choice could have a significant impact on your independence, and potentially put you in a situation from which it may be impossible to recover. I experienced this situation during the first couple of years of living on my own. You quickly learn which things are more important. I always felt better when I made the right, mature decision. Besides, I always got over whatever it was that I was griping about, or the things I couldn't do because of higher priorities.

As I look back on that period of my life, I have an appreciation for my hardships and experiences, which helped to improve my sense of judgment and decision-making. I wouldn't change those experiences, because they taught me the consequences of poor decision-making.

On the flip side, what I *would* change or do differently during that time is to have asked for help when it was really needed.

I didn't believe in asking people for help for several reasons. One, my pride was too great, and I felt uncomfortable asking for help. In a sense, it made me feel like a peasant begging for handouts.

Another reason asking for help didn't come easily for me is because I didn't like being let down or rejected.

Lastly, my motto had always been that, if I couldn't provide whatever I needed, then it just wasn't meant for me to have. I believed part of the responsibility I had was to not depend on anyone for help. I didn't like having to depend on someone or something else.

After experiencing more of life, I have a slightly different view. I think it's okay to ask for help *after* all other options have been exhausted. I realize that you can't always make it without help. By not asking when it's truly needed may mean you'll miss out on opportunities. As long as seeking help isn't the *first option* and you've given it your all, it's wise to ask.

Overall, moving out on my own was the beginning to so much more. For instance, I quickly found willpower and strength I never knew I had. Who would have thought I could be as responsible and disciplined so early on, aside from responsibly handling my motherly duties? I developed patience and saw constant personal growth in myself as I sustained my independence.

I'm proud of myself for stepping out on my own and never looking back.

Key Takeaway from Chapter Eleven

Small sacrifices for lasting rewards.

More Takeaways...

- In establishing independence, I had to revamp my entire way of thinking from what I had been accustomed to.

- I could no longer choose and do things I had done when I had more support.

- Whenever I felt like giving up, I thought about how far I had come and how close I was to the finish line.

- My primary goal out of high school was to use my college degree and work for a company that offered opportunities where I could excel.

- It was a tough decision to work part-time while attending college, so I could keep my head above water financially.

- I felt bad having less time to spend with my son, but I would have felt worse if I couldn't feed and clothe him, and put a roof over his head.

- The sacrifices were temporary so I could get a college education to work smarter, not harder.

TWELVE

Thicker Skin

On paper, it showed I had progressed; yet sometimes, I still felt like that seven-year-old girl who needed her mommy so badly, except I was trapped inside a grown woman's body and had to do what I needed to do to take care of my family, overcome the challenges of my past, and raise my son the best way I knew how.

Growing up, I didn't have the luxury of acting my true age. I had to mature quicker than most kids my age, so that I could take on whatever situations I faced. I had to grow up and accept that I would never receive the love and affection I needed from my parents, so that I could provide love and affection to my siblings. I had to satisfy the sexual desires of others. I had become a mother before my senior prom. It felt like, overnight, I went from being a little girl to a grown woman.

Due to experiences that formed me into the person I had become, I was often perceived as someone who could hold my own, who needed no, or minimal, help. People insinuated that I was tough as nails, or that my heart was cold and empty of emotions. I can only guess these people mistook my experiences and drive for a tough-girl persona. In school, most girls, especially the prissy ones, thought I was a sophisticated version of "hood." To them, I was someone who was very independent and not easily intimidated.

This was weird to me because I couldn't see what others saw. In fact, I thought of myself as the weakest person on earth, someone too afraid to stand up for herself, and who had failed at protecting her sister and brother. For some reason, I was always afraid to say "no" or fight back. I had developed this pattern throughout my childhood and young adult life. I would just give in to whatever fear I had, often doing what I was told, even if I didn't feel comfortable doing it.

After years of timidity and fearfulness, I wondered what strength people saw in me—and *where it was*—because I hadn't a clue. If I had known back then that I was so tough, I may have prevented a lot of pain, hurt, and disappointment for myself.

Contrary to what people may have thought of me, I always felt that my weakness and lack of courage to fight back played a significant role in what happened to me. Simply put, I wasn't *tough enough*. I couldn't find the courage to speak out.

I'm not sure why I would just do what people wanted me to do, but I guess I felt that the path of least resistance was my best option. If I let things happen, maybe they would stop quicker or leave me alone afterwards. Maybe people would accept me and not judge me because of what was happening to me at home and away from home. All I knew was, I didn't want to get hurt anymore, and I was willing to do whatever it took for that not to happen.

Living with troubling experiences made me easily intimidated and feeling inferior to others, at times. Maybe this is what happens to other children or youth living in similar situations. It becomes a pattern to conform or become timid to avoid making matters worse.

Somewhere along the way, I lost the courage to speak my mind or stand up for myself. Sometimes, I just didn't feel like fighting anymore. Sometimes, I was afraid to ask for help—mostly because I was afraid of the consequences it would bring, but also because it didn't seem like there was much help around then compared to today.

Over the past eight years, I've developed a different perspective on toughening up. I believe it was more damaging to me, mentally, when I didn't stand up for myself and for what was right.

I'm no longer afraid of consequences or how others will perceive me. It's more courageous to fight for what I stand for, and for a good cause.

I cannot change the past, and I can no longer allow myself to hide behind it. I am my own individual, an individual who is free to define who she is and not let the ugly reflections of the past define this new person.

My identity reflects the positive direction in which I want my life to go. It reflects the wisdom I've gained, which embodies confidence and resilience. I no longer have the same old fears, because I realize *I* am the only one who can break me. If I want my future to be better than my past, then the choices I make in life, the way that I carry myself, the people that I surround myself with, must all reflect it.

Key Takeaway from Chapter Twelve

Embrace every scar.

More Takeaways...

- Each scar (bad memory) is a reminder of how strong I am today.

- My identity is defined by the positive direction in which I'm taking my life, not by ugly reflections of my past.

- I am the only one who can break me, and I no longer fear how others view me.

- The "keys" that opened my future were the choices I made, the way I carried myself, and the people I surrounded myself with.

- If I want my future to be better than my past, then the choices I make in life, the way that I carry myself, the people that I surround myself with, must all reflect it.

THIRTEEN

Unwilling Circumstances

Kids growing up in disadvantaged households and communities are usually more vulnerable and at risk for dangerous or harmful situations. Parents frequently are absent from home, or preoccupied with things that don't involve caring for their children, thereby leaving their kids exposed to serious harm.

Usually, the harm continues until someone finds out and offers much-needed help. The children or youth may be afraid to go for help, or they may fear what will happen to them if they do. Some may have no one to talk to, so they hold things inside and continue to suffer.

Then there are children who *do* try to get help, but their parents or guardians aren't attentive because of their addictions or substance abuse issues.

If the parents aren't providing protection for their children or youth, these kids may feel there's no one who will protect them. This can lead children to accept or comply when harmful situations arise, because there is no support or protection from their parents. The results are that the harmful circumstances are prolonged.

Some children and young people look on their parents as their ultimate protectors who can keep them safe from harm or danger. When parents fail to protect, the children or youth have less hope that *anyone* can help or protect them. This disappointment of being let down because of parents' failures can be misconstrued to mean that it's okay to go along with whatever the harmful situation may be. Some may even become conflicted and believe the perpetrator has their best interests in mind.

If I could go back in time, I would have done things differently. I would have been more aware, recognizing the signs of my vulnerability. Knowing these signs would have meant making better decisions that would have steered me away from harm. I would have said "no" to more things that I had given into out of peer pressure or influence. I would have talked to someone, rather than keeping things bottled in.

One time in particular that I wish I could have stood up for myself took place in South Bend, Indiana, when I was about eight years old. I was walking to my mother's friend's house with her boys and some other kids. We stopped in an alley along the way, and I was pressured into performing sexual acts with one of the boys. I didn't want to, but I was outnumbered and gave in.

After it happened, I was mad at myself. I hadn't put up a fight or tried to resist. Although we were kids and didn't really understand the enormity of what we were doing, it was yet another moment where I felt violated and taken advantage of, and I felt like a failure. I had failed to stand up to them and say no. It was another missed opportunity to speak up and fight back.

When we first moved to Minnesota, we lived in a shelter in downtown Minneapolis called 410 Shelter. We met another family there who also came from Gary, Indiana. Our mothers became good friends, and we kids formed a bond, too. The other family found a place to live before we did, so we stayed with them for a short time in South Minneapolis.

The woman had a daughter around my age, a son who was around my brother's age, and a daughter near my sister's age. I became good friends with the older daughter, and we hung out a lot. We even remained close friends after we moved into our own place. We often stayed overnight at one another's house where we would hang out and play, or babysit for others and earn money.

I hated staying over when her brother was home, because I was terrified of going to sleep. Several times, he tried to perform sexual acts with me, once everyone else had fallen asleep. I would tell him no and fight him off of me. He'd stop—until I had fallen asleep, that is. I would often wake up to my clothes down around my ankles. I hated him for this and thought he was a disgusting pervert but I never confronted him, because I didn't think it would do any good. I just went on my way the next day as if it hadn't happened. He was sick and truly disgusted me.

There was a time I was visiting my cousin in Northeast Minneapolis. I went to a convenience store not far from her house, and as I was standing in line waiting to pay for my things, two drunken white men walked in. The owner of the store, who was from the Middle East, kept a close eye on them when they became disorderly. Next thing I knew, they were both behind me in line. One of them grabbed my behind and laughed. He said something disgusting and condescending after he had done it. I didn't move or turn around and say something, but I was enraged. I was so angry that they had violated me, I really wished I could hurt them. The store owner witnessed it and yelled at them and told them to get out of the store.

Afterward, I was extremely angry with myself for not speaking up and doing something about it. I couldn't stop thinking about what I *should* have done and the fact that I didn't.

At that moment, I was fed up with being taken advantage of, and vowed I would always fight back and protect myself from then on.

Since then, I've unfortunately become extremely defensive, because I had lacked courage in the past. Now I always have my guard up. I struggle with a proper balance. I've gotten better, but I'm still a work in progress.

Like me, boys, girls, women, and men in similar situations don't fight back, because they don't think it will help. By letting things slide, we're not considering the long-term effect it can have on our lives. I was one of those people living with a lot of regret. I hadn't respected myself enough to fight back or stand up. I took the path of least resistance, because it was easier and, I thought, safer. I didn't understand that path would have a worse effect on me, and possibly cause difficulties later.

If I could go back to the times when I was violated or when I succumbed out of fear or lack of courage, the outcome would be different. I would not allow anyone to violate or pressure me into doing anything against my will, or do things I didn't feel comfortable doing.

But it's not just me I have to think about. By not doing anything about them, these people go on doing these horrible things to others.

I hope that others will use my experience to know that getting help or fighting back can make a difference in their lives and in others' lives.

After each experience, I felt I had let myself down. I didn't feel good about myself because I hadn't even tried. It was like I didn't have enough dignity or self-respect to defend myself. What I didn't understand then was, if I didn't have self-respect, then I shouldn't expect respect from others, either.

Had I defended myself, I believe some of my past situations may have turned out differently. Even if I hadn't succeeded in preventing those things from happening, fighting or speaking up would have helped me feel better about myself, because I would have tried my hardest, and I would have felt stronger by saying no and not giving in to fear or peer pressure.

It's extremely important that we—boys, girls, women, and men—command respect for ourselves, and do our best to prevent anyone from violating us. Our dignity and self-respect are worthwhile and worth fighting for.

Win or lose, we must fight for what is right. If something isn't right, then we must do something about it. We cannot just give in to fear or others' power and influence, but must do everything in our power to command the level of respect we deserve—and not let anyone take it from us.

What matters most is that we try our best; that alone warrants self-respect.

Whether female or male, having a great deal of self-respect and dignity can make a dramatic difference in how people treat you. Your confidence level lets others know you mean business and that you are serious about every aspect of your personal life.

Exuding confidence could make people rethink unethical or impure motives before they act. Specifically, people would be more reluctant to disrespect and violate you, because they would be afraid you would not give in to their demands. This is especially true for people who try to force others to do things against their will. Self-confidence may also influence others to hold you in higher regard and influence the way they treat you in general.

When someone violates you, or shows a lack of respect, show them what respect looks like by respectfully defusing the situation or walking away. It's best to not respond or react in a hostile way; that could make matters worse.

Sometimes, self-respect means simply walking away to minimize a situation before it escalates. It does *not* mean putting yourself or others in danger. Some people may not have it in them to respect others. Those are issues that we cannot and should not try to change on our own.

Getting respect from others isn't always easy. Unfortunately, the world is filled with people who will attempt to disrespect or violate others if they can. Someone who's often been victimized may become unnecessarily defensive and combative, and not realize it. Demanding respect doesn't mean you have to be aggressive, it simply means not accepting any demoralizing or dehumanizing behavior toward you; not allowing yourself to be victimized in any way.

After reaching my breaking point, I became extremely guarded and defensive to the extent that I would sometimes become more confrontational than defensive. I vowed that I would fight back and not allow fear to take control and cause me to give in to pressure or harmful circumstances. I would stand up for what was right, whether it was inflicted on others or me. I would no longer play it safe by keeping silent. Never again did I want to walk away feeling I hadn't fought for myself, or thinking later about what I *should* have done.

Eventually, I became overly defensive in demanding respect and not being violated. Unaware of what was happening within me, I became extremely sensitive, paranoid, and combative for the slightest reasons, believing that most people had bad intentions.

I wasn't good at picking my battles, or discerning if I was over-analyzing a situation and misinterpreting the person's intent. Sometimes when I became overly defensive or protective, I made matters worse by painting a negative image of me and missing opportunities.

I struggled to find the right balance to defend myself in constructive ways. I realize now I had allowed a few bad experiences to influence my reactions to everything. Those bad experiences clouded my judgment. I wasn't thinking clearly and handling things respectfully or rationally. I was always afraid that someone was trying to hurt me, or they were out to get me.

I had to learn how to react cautiously and stay open-minded when feeling disrespected. I began taking more time to think about situations from various angles. Conscientiously remaining calm and rational, things turn out better. I stopped making situations worse by being confrontational and missing opportunities. As a result, I was respected more as a person, and that's always the ultimate goal.

Key Takeaway from Chapter Thirteen

Use your strength.

More Takeaways...

- Courageously standing up for what you believe in may help others who may be going through similar circumstances.

- Even if you don't win the battle, just standing up for yourself is a victory.

- What matters most is that you tried your best, and that alone warrants self-respect.

FOURTEEN

Hiding Behind Walls

Ever since I can remember, opening up to people was one of my biggest fears and produced lots of anxiety. Engaging with others is an inevitable part of life, yet I was so uncomfortable and on edge most of the time. Because I spent so much time alone when I was placed in temporary living, I had become accustomed to keeping to myself, rarely interacting or engaging with others.

Even in the foster homes or shelters I was in, letting people in wasn't easy. My state of mind didn't let me feel it was okay, or that I could trust that no harm would come to me by doing so. They weren't my family, and only my family could make me feel okay. My mother and siblings knew me very well, and I felt secure with them. They were all I knew and longed for, at the time. I didn't know anyone in those other places, or what they were capable of. Getting acclimated to new surroundings again was unsettling. That old and comfortable familiarity was gone for the time-being, and I sometimes felt lonely and abandoned.

To escape the discomfort and desolation of these places, I sought a peaceful place where no one would intrude. Most times, that meant being by myself, in my room, away from others. It eventually became the norm, and I used it as a defense mechanism in various situations.

For a brief time, my biological father moved to Minnesota from Rochester, New York, to attempt to become sober. If he changed environments, he thought, he may have a better chance at sobriety.

Initially, he stayed with me and my son in my apartment. I

thought it would be a good idea and would give us an opportunity to form the daddy-daughter relationship I'd always fantasized about; a moment I longed for all my life. I was excited that it could finally be possible, depending, of course, on whether he became sober permanently.

Soon, I realized my hope was short-lived. He didn't become sober, as he said he would; he was drunk all the time, and that terrified me. I didn't know him well enough to be living with him while he was drunk.

Every day he was there, I would come home from work and stay in my room, because I felt uncomfortable being around him. He had the living room area all to himself. I felt like a prisoner in my own home. He told my brother that he felt I didn't want him there, because I was always avoiding him, and he was right. I didn't want him there. I was angry that he would do this.

For one thing, I don't allow excessive drinking or any type of drugs to be done in my home. For another, he had promised me he would do better and stop drinking.

And last, all my hopes and dreams of having a sober father and a loving relationship with my daddy went out the window. I called my brother and told him this wasn't going to work, and that he had to come get our father.

My brother took him to stay at his house because he knew I was having a hard time with him at my house, especially when he was drunk. He stayed with my brother and his family for a while, and then he checked himself into a treatment program in Minneapolis. He became sober. I saw him at church on a regular basis with members of the treatment program. He stuck it out for a while in Minnesota, but eventually moved back to where he had lived in New York, with our family. He began drinking again, and I didn't have a consistent relationship with him.

I kept to my goal, advancing within my career field. I also worked on opening up more, and not getting discouraged when I was in a new environment with new or unfamiliar people. My goal was to break the mold of feeling afraid or inferior because of my past. However, seeing my parents continue to suffer from substance abuse made it challenging for me to accomplish this. I no longer wanted other people's perceptions of me to weigh me down or bother me.

I worked on not allowing the scars and memories from my past to linger in my present life, or follow me into my future. When I was in environments similar to those in my past, I wanted being there not to have an effect on me. I wanted to reach a point where I no longer valued myself less because others had different experiences than mine.

I also wanted to stop being afraid of how people would judge me based on things I had no control over, or things I did without understanding their full impact. I just wanted to be okay, wherever I was and whomever I was with. To do this, I looked for opportunities that took me out of my comfort zone and gave me the chance to face my fears of being open and inviting to others.

As part of these efforts, I took a work trip that provided room and board for leaders in training. Fellow employees also took classes, all at the same location.

I had a difficult time adjusting. The longer I was there, the more overcome I was with emotion. Our location had been compared to a five-star hotel and well-known for its outstanding customer service.

About 35 people attended the workshop I was in, along with instructors. Everyone was friendly, and we were all there to learn. One couldn't ask for a better place to spend five days—except me, that is.

One of the most challenging moments was the time I spent in my room. In a sense, it was like a luxury dorm room. But, for some reason, it reminded me of the children's shelter I once lived in. Its similarities took me back to when I was away from home in a place I didn't want to be in.

Even the layout of this facility had parallels to the group home, and it unsettled me. There was a dining area where all the guests ate breakfast, lunch, and dinner, which was like the one at the group home. Guests could visit activity rooms between or after classes, and they were similar to the ones at the group home, too. The establishment was also surrounded by woods. When I looked out of the window in my room, I was taken back to when I looked out of the window in my room in the group home, times when I would be thinking how badly I wanted out of that place and to be at home with my family.

Being there brought back sad memories that made it difficult for me to enjoy my stay, or to completely focus on why I was there.

After class ended for the day, most people hung out in the lounge and entertainment areas, to drink and to network. They laughed together, played games, and had fun.

I mostly went straight to my room until it was time for dinner. I dreaded mealtime, because that meant I had to share a table with complete strangers and socialize.

It reminded me of the shelter where I sat alone or at tables with kids I didn't know who were there because their circumstances were like mine. The cafeteria was where you could see all the kids living in the shelter in one place; kids who lived in wings separated by age group. Unfortunately, I could see kids, especially the younger ones, who were hurting just as I was, and missing their families. It bothered me most because I was a big sister, and it would devastate me to see my sister in that place.

It's not that the shelter made me feel threatened or unsafe in any way, because the adults running the facility did the best they could to create an environment where kids felt comfortable.

But the reality of it was that the people working in the cafeteria and with the kids were *just doing a job*. They weren't there to provide kids with the love and affection they were missing or needed. All they could do was tell them where to sit and when to get up. That wasn't even remotely close to the type of supervision we kids needed, even at mealtime. I needed my mom, my sister, and my brother, and I can imagine the other kids may have been feeling the same way. It often made mealtimes sad, watching as the younger kids struggled to get adjusted. Sometimes, they just looked sad, lost, or lonely.

It was psychological torture as I sat in the cafeteria of the leadership training facility. Planning for this work trip, I hadn't anticipated that something as simple as mealtime would make me so uncomfortable and uneasy.

I guess a few of my fellow class members noticed I didn't participate in group activities. Some of them went out of their way to make me feel comfortable and a part of the group. None of them had a clue to my internal struggles.

On the last day, we all had to give a presentation on the information we learned, and how we planned to apply it to our day-to-day routines. Who would have thought something so simple and harmless, and something I have done many, many times before, would have been so challenging for me? I often put together presentations and gave them while in college or at work, so this was nothing new.

This time, it was different. Overcome with emotion, I apologized to the class and instructors for being so closed off.

I could no longer fight back the tears. Before I realized it, I was explaining why it was difficult for me to be more open. I was lost. I managed to get through it and deliver my presentation. Most of my classmates empathized with me and were overcome with sorrow, as well.

I learned from this experience that my wounds go deeper than I had imagined. I needed to get help addressing some of these issues that I'd managed to keep bottled up. Some of these things hindered me from moving forward, and I hadn't realized it until I went to this workshop.

Basically, being alone had become my safe haven. Over the years, I became accustomed to, preferred, and sought isolation as a sense of comfort and security.

As I advanced in my professional career, networking events were always a challenge for me. Regardless of what I had accomplished, I didn't feel it separated me from the adversities of my life growing up. I wasn't a huge socialite, and meeting new people or talking to strangers wasn't one of my strengths. Mingling made me uneasy, as if I didn't fit in or as if I was an outcast.

I found myself overcompensating by trying to act "normal," portraying myself as someone who has had it easy her whole life. I was trying too hard to fit in, and it felt pretentious and silly. It's why being alone became so much easier for me. It doesn't require nearly as much work or effort. At times, normalcy felt like obscurity. I wasn't sure if my wounds or memories would ever allow me to feel normal.

I worried that the stigma of past experiences was all too obvious to others, as if those experiences had become a permanent scar on the outside for all to see. I worried that people could tell that I grew up in poverty, suffered physical and sexual abuse, had drug-addicted parents, and that I had grown up in a broken home.

So, typically at social events, I found a way to fade to the back where I interacted less with people. The less I had to introduce myself and talk with people, the less they knew about me. I was afraid of those tough questions people generally ask as they get to know about you and what you do. No matter how hard I tried to steer the conversation in another direction, curious people never failed to ask how I got to be where I was. Questions like: where was I born, what did my parents do, do I have any children, how old are they, was I married to the father, and on and on. I dreaded those questions. When people heard my answers, I feared they'd form judgments, and they wouldn't be good ones.

I tried not to let these things bother me—after all, I hadn't become those things of my past—but, sometimes, I wasn't successful in avoiding this feeling.

One would think that going to so many events would get easier with time. Well, that wasn't the case for me. As long as I carried unhealed wounds, the less I could feel confident that people wouldn't see them.

Self-respect and dignity are catalysts for defining oneself. These two characteristics help build confidence and self-worth. People who think highly of themselves are not easily intimidated. We often worry too much about how others perceive us. We let their perceptions discourage us or discredit all that we have worked so hard to achieve and become.

I was that person who felt insecure around certain crowds—afraid of the labels and judgments society places on people with my background. I've always felt that I had to work harder than the ordinary person because of my upbringing.

What I *didn't* know was that those things don't define who I am. They are a *part* of me, they influenced some of my decisions (the good and the bad), but they don't define who I am. That part is all up to me.

By watching others who I knew had come from humble beginnings, I learned that where I'm from doesn't determine where I end up in life. So many people with far better upbringings than mine have ended up worse off. One would think that, since they had a leg up, they would have become something greater. I quickly learned this is not always the case. It has more to do with making the best out of what we have and opportunities we've been given.

Over time, I've learned that worrying about what others think of me only holds me back from achieving my goals. Worry demoralizes my self-esteem and all that I've worked hard to be and not be. I figured out that, as long as I am content within myself and have embraced my early life experiences as just a part of my past, I could give a rat's ass about how others perceive me.

Everyone comes from different walks of life. My difference is what makes me unique, and it's a wonderful thing! My past proves that, if I can overcome such obstacles, I can conquer *anything I set my mind to*. That, to me, is the greatest self-respect I could give myself. I am no longer afraid of those tough questions, the reality being that the answers are the reasons *why I am qualified* to be in a similar or higher position professionally. It's why I am in the same room with all the others at networking events, and why I have a seat at the table of like-minded or prominent figures.

So, in the future, I have vowed to answer the tough questions with dignity and pride.

Key Takeaway from Chapter Fourteen

Embrace the past.

More Takeaways...

- To move in a positive direction, I had to acknowledge that my wounds went deeper than I had realized.

- The longer I allowed the wounds to go unresolved, the less confident I was about my future.

- I made a conscientious effort to not allow past scars and memories to spill into my future.

- I sought opportunities that helped me address my challenges, so they were no longer a problem for me.

- I learned to embrace the past and to use the problems to aid me in making informed and healthy decisions.

- My past and the lessons I've learned are the reasons for my success today.

FIFTEEN

Epiphany

Some people may not realize how their past can affect their future. They may think that time and those events have passed, and they do not expect them to resurface. Some of us try shutting out or erasing those experiences, thinking that it's easier to deal with the memories by *not* dealing with them, or to go through life pretending nothing ever happened. Eventually, we end up living in those times, without being aware of it, and suffer long after the trauma happened.

Suffering comes in many forms and affects us all differently. It may be in the way we interact with people, the friends or companions we choose, or the way we handle current situations based on their similarity to past situations. Some of us may not realize this is occurring and have difficulty acknowledging it's a problem, or that our past still haunts us.

People suffering over past trauma become defensive when confronted with it, or are in disbelief—it's a state of denial because we don't want to face past trauma. It feels so much easier to close things off, to forget about it.

But it's not healthy, and can lead to more emotional damage down the line.

Coping with unfortunate circumstances can be difficult for some who may feel there is no resolution or cure for overcoming these experiences. It may seem impossible to get to a place where the memories aren't as painful or melancholy. Life seems better when you forget about the past or pretend it never existed, because you escape from such a dark period to a happier, less-stressful time.

That is, until the past resurfaces. "Don't associate yourself with the past and your future should be so much brighter," some say. For others, our past appears to be a nonissue; but, the reality is that it's there and it hinders us from fully recovering.

I was never one to be victimized by my past, or to use it as an excuse for my actions. I judged people who did that and felt they used past tragic events as an easy way out. I felt that, too often and too easily, licensed psychiatrists, therapists, etc., diagnosed their patients based on past experiences, which opened the doors to excuse themselves and not be accountable for their actions or choices.

My motto has always been, that if a person knows right from wrong and understands the consequences of their actions, they were in their right frame of mind to make conscious decisions. I could never understand why this concept isn't taken into consideration and why our society excuses people from the bad choices they make, or blames their behavior on a past experience or trauma, or gives some other indefensible excuse.

It wasn't until recently that I began seeing a pattern in my own behavior. Looking back at the events that took place, I can see a correlation between those events and my life today. I guess I'd been naïve. As I mature, I realize that events or trauma can indirectly impact a person, and influence behavior and choices.

Although I can't pinpoint specific event(s), I realize some still affect me now. The following incidents most likely played a part in my development: whining and longing for attention, isolating myself, not opening up to people, my commitment phobia, feeling that "harsh" and "raw" is the best way to learn, and becoming emotional when I see disadvantaged youth or adults with substance abuse problems.

They're all reminders of my past.

All these things (the good and the bad) have contributed to the person I am today. If I failed to see the correlation before, I see it now. However, I try to be aware of it when making certain decisions. I work hard not to let my past negatively influence my present, and to use those experiences as learning opportunities in making better decisions.

It's common practice to allow the past into the present. It's usually because we naturally gravitate toward what we've experienced, what we're familiar with—whether it's good or bad. We subconsciously look for similar characteristics from our past, or for things we lacked that we felt we needed.

Growing up without a father in the home, or with a parent having substance abuse problems, can cause development issues that will likely carry into adulthood.

These abnormal experiences can greatly influence the choices we make, and they can control us. They can cause us to become accustomed to things similar to how we grew up. Maybe it's unhealthy relationships, accepting single parenting as a normal way of life, experimenting with drugs, being timid or afraid to soar and spread our wings, or feeling like a caged bird, and so much more. If we're not mindful of these things, conscious of our past, then we may be destined to return to that place we've tried to escape, and endure more pain and suffering.

Unfortunately, some of my past has hardened me to where I don't let my hair down to be as free as I would like. My past has made it challenging for me to open up and let people in, or get the help I need. I'm extremely reticent when it comes to sharing things about myself, especially my personal feelings and experiences. I've built a shell around my feelings to protect who I am, and to suppress the negatives, so that people won't judge me or look down on me.

My past experiences have hardened me to where I feel that the best way to learn is to hear it in the harshest and rawest form. That method has taught me to not sugarcoat or lighten the blow, but to present the harsh reality, which is the only way people will "get it." I've learned that the softer, subtler approach won't be taken seriously.

I've lived by this model, and it's what my immediate family and closest friends see. However, it's caused a strain between me and some of my loved ones. With good intentions, I hold my loved ones to higher expectations, just as I do for myself. I feel I should be just as hard and critical on them as I am on myself.

My brother once told me that I can't expect everyone to do things the way I do them, or with the same degree of urgency, tenacity, or drive. Although I meant well and gave positive and constructive feedback, sometimes the way I delivered the feedback came off too strong. I certainly wasn't indicating they were beneath me—*just different from me.*

I never intended to insult anyone or have them walk away feeling hurt. I just wanted to share experiences that had allowed me to learn from my mistakes. I also thought giving it to them raw and uncut now could save them from learning the hard way after it was too late.

I used to think that if *I* could turn my life around, then *anyone* could. I felt that because I lived in corrupt environments, became an adolescent parent, and lacked any positive role models—that anyone who grew up in a better situation had a greater chance of succeeding than I did. There shouldn't be any excuses for them not to.

It wasn't until I was an adult that I learned not everyone has the same degree of motivation and ambition. What fueled my motivation may not be what fuels others' motivation. That's neither good nor bad, just different.

Some people may not know what it's like to go without food, to be subject to abuse, or to wear the same clothes every day, so their sense of urgency may not be the same as mine. That doesn't make one any less than the other.

I'm learning that my approach isn't always the best, and that I can't expect what works for me to be what works for others. This is what makes us different, and that's okay. My style and approach are likely the result of how I grew up. I'm harsh and super-critical because sometimes life was that way to me.

This may be yet another example of me being unaware of my past affecting my present.

If I learned anything from giving "constructive criticism" to my loved ones, it's that the way I view things may not be the reality of their situation. It isn't up to me to decide how harsh a message needs to be delivered for them to get it; the way I think things may turn out isn't necessarily the *only way* they'll turn out. Although my intentions were pure and without malice, I've failed to give positive reinforcement if that person feels attacked or I've put them down. It's become my mission to be more uplifting, versus giving worst-case scenarios.

In putting my past behind me and looking to the future, it occurred to me that I may be holding onto resentment and pain from being hurt by others. I had unrealistic expectations that people would naturally treat others according to how they want to be treated. I didn't know how to process that we, as humans, aren't perfect and that we're capable of hurting others. Only recently have I realized that I need to learn how to talk about things that hurt me and to forgive and move forward, rather than harbor the pain.

Had I known then what I know now, my burden could have been lightened. I could have had a better relationship with my parents. I could have been more open and sociable and not felt inferior to others.

Sometimes, it feels like I've been carrying every wound I ever received for 30-plus years, because I hadn't found a way to let go or allowed the wounds to heal. As a result, some of my interactions may have reflected the pain and disappointment.

More recently, I've realized I must forgive myself, and those who have offended me, to let go of the oppression that taunts me. I must channel my inner strength to let go of the pain and anger.

It may also help me to face my pain and fears by accepting and acknowledging them. I must embrace the things that I've held onto for so long, and understand that I can't change what happened. I must get to a good place while living with the pain and fears. This may be a useful coping mechanism when I'm reminded of those times, and it may help put some closure to them.

Some of what we go through becomes a permanent part of us, but we don't have to let them define who we grow up to be. The first step to recovery is to acknowledge what has happened and to face those things head on. Then, get them out in the open and talk about the things that have been fomenting inside of us for so long.

It may also be beneficial to look for correlations linking to our past, acknowledging if we are still living in the past and allowing those events to influence the present.

I'm learning that being reminded of my past isn't necessarily a bad thing. It could save me from making poor decisions that might lead to pain, heartache, and mistakes. It could improve the way I think, make choices, and how I interact and communicate with others.

Not everything has to be in the *harshest, rawest form*. By accepting my past and learning to deal with it in a positive way, I'm improving my well-being and helping myself live a healthier, more prosperous life.

Those past experiences have become lessons and opportunities versus a way of life.

Key Takeaway from Chapter Fifteen

*What works for me may not work for others,
and that's okay.*

More Takeaways...

- Avoiding problems or sensitive issues won't make them go away, but talking about them helps to manage them and/or find resolution.

- Holding on to the past may be why I react to certain situations.

- Life doesn't always go according to how I view it, or what I've experienced.

- Everyone deals with problems in their own way, and that doesn't make one way better than another.

- In providing constructive feedback, deliver the message in such a way that it doesn't cause the person to feel attacked or demoralized.

- I can't change what happened in the past, but I can control how it affects others around me.

SIXTEEN

Is Anyone Listening?

When I was a child, I often felt like I wasn't being heard. I felt that my mother didn't hear my cries, or that I didn't yell loud enough. I felt that my biological father and stepfather weren't paying attention when I shared my concerns about my mother with them, such as how I: pleaded with my mother to stay sober and clean, told her how it affected us when she didn't, and needed her and loved her.

I also wasn't being heard when I visited my biological father, told him about the situation at home, and that I wanted to live with him. He did nothing about that, either.

It didn't seem like what I was saying was enough to get their attention. Something drastic would have to happen to me before they would hear me. Naturally, I became the designated spokesperson for my brother, sister, and me by having repeated conversations with my mom on how she affected us when she got high, or when she left us alone for long periods of time, or when she became intoxicated and violent.

These conversations were my cries for help and for my mom to get help, but they fell on deaf ears.

When people aren't being heard by their loved ones, especially when something is wrong, people can often feel powerless or invisible. They tend to shut down, suppress their feelings, and not seek help. They grow accustomed to their environment and live in unhealthy or unsafe conditions.

What would it take before someone heard me? Did I need to go to extremes, like inflict pain on myself? Did I need to be in danger before someone stopped and listened or took me seriously? Did my parents care enough about me to listen or address my concerns?

It was sad for me, because I tried to get help the only way I really knew how, from the only people I thought could help. It just didn't seem like anyone cared enough. I hoped that, by telling my mother and father how their choices were hurting us, they would stop and listen. But I quickly learned that it went in one ear and out the other. I had very little hope.

I often thought that expressing myself in different ways would make a difference. If I acted out in a certain way, would that capture their attention and be my opportunity to get the help we all needed? If I spoke in the dialect of my feelings—anger and frustration—or sang songs of sorrow and pain, then would someone hear me? I wondered what it took to be a gangster, and could I be one? Does a gangster have to be big, tough, and feared by others? Sell drugs, kill, or be in a gang?

There were times when I wanted to become a gangster rapper just to release some of my frustration and anger. I figured it would give me toughness to hide behind, and I'd be inferior to nothing and nobody. I mostly wanted to rap about the struggle that has plagued our nation for decades in the inner cities and in poverty-stricken homes, or what it was like growing up in Gary, Indiana (murder capital) in a household with two drug-addicted parents, constantly lacking the necessities to survive, but always finding a way.

I often hear rappers rap about the street hustle, but I wanted to rap about the hustle of life as a female growing up in less-fortunate circumstances, making my way out of no way, rising above, and helping others do the same. To me, that was more appealing than taking a bullet or shooting at someone, selling drugs, joining a gang, or intimidating others. Overcoming situations and circumstances that are out of our control, versus street life activity, which can be prevented and avoided if a person really wants to.

Having the strength and courage to survive uncontrollable situations demonstrates credibility that should be highly respected, more so than a gun-toting, blunt-smoking, pants-sagging, drug-selling street thug.

This should be the tough reputation one should want to be known and admired for: someone whose trials and tribulations made them stronger and more prepared for future challenges and obstacles; someone who is resilient and able to bounce back from post-traumatic experiences and be a testimony to inspire others; someone who turns their negative experiences into learning opportunities by finding the good in the bad. Now, *that's gangster* and *worth rapping about*!

I wanted to be the female version of Tupac Shakur, as I tell my version of "Brenda's Having A Baby" or "Dear Mama." It would be interesting to know how many can attest to similar situations and rap about how they overcame them without resorting to violence or drugs. Unfortunately, I'll bet we would learn that more, rather than fewer, have succumbed to and become a product of their surroundings. My rap song would be for survivors and positive leaders who helped their communities overcome the vicious cycle of repeating the sins passed down from generation to generation!

At other times, I've wanted to sing gospel in church, to scream at the top of my lungs, thanking God for pulling me through challenging times, having mercy and bestowing grace on me, and for being that sounding board when I needed someone to talk to.

I guess my main goal was to vocalize my pain and triumphs, in hopes of lifting this huge burden off my shoulders, a burden I've carried with me for years. It didn't matter to me *how* I voiced my pain and triumphs, just as long as I had a platform to do it.

Since singing and rapping aren't my forte, I chose to take on a literary approach to express my feelings, hoping it would provide some therapy. I've always enjoyed writing, and it's made a tremendous impact on my life, past and present.

In addition to writing about my life in 5th grade, I did make another attempt in high school.

My 11th grade English teacher, Mr. Roberts, announced a writing contest being put on by a local university. The topic had been preselected and contestants were expected to write to the topic. I really enjoyed writing, so, of course I opted in, only I didn't write about the topic chosen for contestants. I wrote about my life and how it had evolved since the last time I wrote about it. I turned in my multipage essay and waited to hear back.

Similar to my 5th-grade teacher's response, my English teacher was touched by my story and shared it with other faculty members. He also told me that my essay was selected by the judges as one of the best stories submitted for the contest. I didn't win the contest because I hadn't written about the chosen topic, but I did win an honorable mention. I attended the award ceremony at the college and I received my certificate in front of a large audience.

After that experience, I realized that writing about my life was not only therapeutic for me but also interesting to others. People like hearing stories about people overcoming obstacles and beating the odds. It also dawned on me that if my words had such an effect on these few people, perhaps they could have an even more profound effect on those in similar situations. Maybe my experiences could inspire or help someone to make better choices or overcome any oppression they may be dealing with.

Both writing experiences made it clear to me that, even if I wasn't being heard at home, I *was* being heard by teachers, principals, and other faculty members. In a way, maybe I was asking for help and didn't know that's what I was doing. It was nice to receive recognition and encouragement and to see that others did care and were willing to help.

Bottom line is that people are listening. Don't keep quiet or stop trying to be heard because you're not getting the response you want from the people you feel should react. Perhaps it's because they need a voice to cry out for them, too, and your cry for help just may be it. You may not only receive help for yourself, but for others, too.

Key Takeaway from Chapter Sixteen

Use your voice.

More Takeaways…

- Writing was my platform to be heard, to find closure, and to seek help.

- Writing and journaling may not only be therapy for you, but a way to get help for others, too.

- Don't get discouraged and give up because someone hasn't responded or reacted as quickly as you had hoped.

Role Model

In junior high school, some of the younger kids looked up to me as if I was someone cool. They seemed impressed with me and were interested in knowing me. Although these girls were younger than me, we looked alike in a lot of ways. They reminded me of how I looked at their age, when I was going through tough times at home, and this connection naturally drew me to them. When they saw me in the halls or during lunch period, they'd go out of their way to speak with me, or even hug me.

I'm not sure what they admired about me, but I believe they may have felt a connection in our lives outside of school. Perhaps I appeared to them as someone who had overcome what they were going through at the time. I could identify with them, so I made it a point to become friends.

I could see the parallels in our lives by the way they dressed, the expressions on their faces, and by their general appearance. That's how I had looked and dressed, like I lacked the financial means to buy decent attire.

Their clothes looked run down or secondhand, much like mine were. Some of the girls had younger siblings who went to the school, as well. When I saw them together, I'd be sad for them, wishing I could do something to help them. It reminded me of me and my siblings and our regular hardships. I wouldn't wish that life on anyone, so it broke my heart to see them this way.

During lunch period, I could see how they eagerly anticipated eating lunch. They looked thankful as they devoured their food, a look and feeling that was all too familiar. I presumed that their lunch satisfied their hunger because they hadn't eaten breakfast and may not have eaten a balanced meal the night before. I, too, lived with these same conditions, and advised the girls about making good choices and not being a follower.

The way they looked up to me reminded me of how I looked up to and admired a few ladies in my neighborhood. To some extent, these ladies had a profound impact on the type of young woman I wanted to become. I admired the way they carried themselves, the quality and treatment they commanded from the men they dated. I admired how they were go-getters, and I admired their independence, their tenacity and their grace. They didn't rely on anyone to take care of them. Each quality inspired me in different ways. I learned from them that one of the most beautiful traits a woman can possess isn't just her looks, but her independence and being a go-getter.

To me, they were bona fide queens who had it going on, and that is the type of queen I aspired to be.

The commonality among the three who influenced me most was their beauty, ambition, class, and their drive to secure the finer things in life. They were the type of women who grabbed attention when they walked into a room. These ladies, who kept jobs, worked hard, and played even harder. They were highly sought after and admired by others during my youth. Whomever they dated had to be just as motivated as they were, and have equal or greater drive and ambition. They didn't settle. They carried themselves with such grace and fineness.

Watching them inspired me to be about my business and to set goals, so that I could afford and sustain certain qualities and standards for myself.

My admiration for these ladies was only a small part of my aspirations to create a better future for myself. They inspired me from a womanly perspective, but I (and my sister and brother) still lacked a full-time, positive figure in my day-to-day life.

Although our family has several prominent people, we didn't regularly see or interact with them, due to distance. My siblings and I pretty much had to figure out this thing called life on our own. We had to rely on our common sense, our faith, and real-life experiences, not on our parents, only to repeat the mistakes they made. I always knew there was a better way to live and that the way we were living wasn't it.

It would have been nice to have a positive influence to guide me and my siblings and offer words of wisdom.

I must say that *witnessing what my mother did and the consequences of her actions* was just as good. Watching her had the same effect as if someone was there to guide me. Some of the choices she was making made me want better for myself. Even though I didn't know quite *how* I'd achieve it, I was confident I *would* make it happen. As long as I believed in me, my sister had all that she needed in a role model. I knew my better choices and decisions would directly impact her, as well.

I may have managed to create a role model for myself within myself, but I can't help but wish that my brother had done the same. It was tougher for him, because he was always the protector. He also was the one who suffered, firsthand, from any abuse before I would.

All the men in our lives were either strung out on drugs or alcohol, or they were jailbirds or deadbeat fathers. The role model pickings for my brother were slim to none. I wish there had been a male figure who had taken him under his wing and guided him to manhood. I wish he had had someone to teach him the things a man should know and do as they mature.

The only influences he had were a father who spent the early part of his life in prison and who went back to be a stone-cold alcoholic when released, and a stepfather who was addicted to drugs and alcohol and was just as abusive as our biological father had been to our mother. My brother only had to pick his poison in choosing between the two.

For the most part, my brother held everything in, and he very seldom showed emotion. For him to show any emotion, something would have to hurt him extremely bad. He was hardly fazed by the things that went on around us, unless they directly affected either of us.

My brother was more forgiving and lenient than I was. He could get over our mother's or stepfather's substance abuse incidents much quicker than I could. He had lifelong problems with his teeth after the traumatic incident with my mother, and he still found a way to forgive her and love her as if it had never happened.

Regardless of what had taken place, by the next day, he usually would be back to loving them unconditionally (unlike me). I was the one who held grudges or let things fester for a long time, because I felt they, as parents, knew better, and I expected better.

My brother had to find ways to adapt to our circumstances at the time, and he didn't have the luxury of thinking far into the future. He was busy protecting my sister and me and didn't take time out to think about and plan his future. He also didn't have adequate tools and resources to do so. Unlike me; he provided me with enough security and stability so that I could think beyond our surroundings to envision a better life.

It's always been my goal to get his teeth repaired, as a small token of my appreciation for him being my big brother and protector. That could just as easily have been me that day, but he stepped up and fought back for all of us. In the end, he paid the price.

The saying, "You never know who's watching you," is something I've learned to be true. We don't get to pick who does and doesn't watch us. That's why it's extremely important to me to do your best, because *you* may be the inspiration or hope for others and not even know it.

Others close by or far from you may be observing what you do and taking notes, because they have no one they can depend on to guide them in a better direction. This is how it was for me as an adolescent and young adult. I admired seeing women become successful and establish their own independence. It gave me hope and inspiration that, one day, that would be me, too. Having someone to look up to is extremely important to some people.

So many of us are inundated with calamity and negativity because of our environment and because we may not be able to afford better. Or maybe our age or some other limitation causes us to live in an environment polluted and saturated with poverty, violence, and few opportunities for advancement. Environments where the highlights and major milestones of one's life are getting a welfare check, getting approval for subsidized housing, dropping out of school, or having children out of wedlock. Conversely, some of us feel the need to surround ourselves with like-minded people, especially when, day-to-day, we're mostly around people who think vastly different.

It's easy to get derailed by what's consistently in front of us, and that's why it's important to expand our world beyond our surroundings and find a different perspective that a positive role model can provide to us. It's especially important when that someone has had similar experiences and has successfully overcome challenges by doing something positive and constructive.

It's easy for people who've never walked in our shoes to offer constructive feedback and guidance, but it doesn't always feel as authentic as someone who's *lived* through it.

Having said that, it can be valuable to get advice from someone with different life experiences, who can offer positive guidance from his or her perspective.

If someone is fortunate enough to have a role model, they should take advantage of the support and resources they can provide. It's better to have positive support and influence than not.

By the same token, a role model isn't a book of answers. They're merely an avenue for guidance, advice, and opportunities. Someone to share your goals and aspirations with and from whom to get support and encouragement. We still have to put in the work ourselves. It's up to us to use these opportunities as stepping stones, but we must act on our own.

In an ideal world, we would be surrounded by positive people to influence us; people we could look up to as leaders or role models. Unfortunately, this is not always a reality.

Many people in this world haven't had the privilege of having a role model, or even the opportunity to meet one. Maybe they don't have the resources to meet people outside of their situation. Their ability to engage in activities outside of their community may be limited, or maybe they lack support at home to connect with positive influencers. Or maybe it's uncommon where they're from and they have no one to pave the way.

In some less-fortunate communities, there may not be many affluent people they can relate to or reach out to for advocacy. In cases like these, they need to think outside the box and dare to be different to create their own positive existence.

To regularly envision life outside of their daily existence is one way to make positive changes—not to mention believing that they can have better.

To regularly think differently about their choices and not be negatively influenced is another important step.

To regularly be open to meeting people from diverse backgrounds and experiences and to learn from them; to become involved in activities outside of their community that challenge them and open doors that create opportunities; to set new goals with plans for achieving them.

These are all doable, important ways to make lasting changes to one's life to have a better future. Taking these steps will help change their mindsets to live for their future and achieve their goals by defining their actions and the decisions that guide them.

This approach has helped me to persevere and reach my goals.

But, it's not for everyone. Some may need a mentor who will

help guide them in a positive direction. If this is a better choice, I would encourage people to look within their school, churches, or youth organizations. I received a ton of support from teachers, principals, and faculty members who all played a big role in sparking my motivation. These people resources are often glad to help youth and young adults get ahead. I've learned that they appreciate the trust and opportunity given to them to lend a helping hand. They're excited for us and anticipate our success, just as much as we do.

A word of caution: In seeking a role model or advocate, be aware that there are people we should *never* allow ourselves to be inspired or influenced by—other than to be inspired or influenced *not* to follow in their footsteps. They're shining examples of what *not to be*.

Growing up in communities where poverty, drugs, and crimes are rampant leaves very few choices for finding role models. My brother wasn't so lucky. Most of what he saw were things that would lead him to a dead end or down the wrong path. What those non-role models' lives have become, through their poor choices, should influence us to never repeat the same mistakes and to want better for ourselves.

Children and young adults need positive guidance and influence, but, at the same time, they need to stay away from people who can never guide them down the right path. It's important to know good direction from bad.

We may be confused and caught up in a lifestyle because it's all we know, and we're not able to see beyond that lifestyle. So, it becomes easy to look up to those around us and think it's okay to be like them. So many people today have been unfortunately misguided in this way. Although it's true that "you have to know better to do better," sometimes knowing better means knowing *what **not** to do*.

As we got older, I tried to be a voice of reason for my brother and to provide constructive criticism. I also tried to act as a positive influence to show him there is a better way going forward. I've always had high expectations for my brother, and I remind him of that as often as I can.

I've tried my best to be there for him when he needed me, and for those times when he didn't. I've always felt I had to make up for the parental guidance we lacked, and for the huge responsibility our parents placed on him as our big brother.

This type of support for one another went both ways. In addition to me being there for him, he was there for me as best as he could. He has always been my rock. Whenever I felt weak, he was there to make me strong. Courtesy of negligent parents, he was the father figure in my life.

We have had our issues, but we've always had each other's back. Although he gets on my nerves, sometimes, he's always there when I really need him. I think he forgets I'm not his daughter. Similarly, I forget I'm not my sister's mother.

I'm not sure how different his life would be if he had had someone to look up to as a child, but I'm certain he wants the best for his children. He never wants them to have the same experiences we had. He makes it his duty to be present in their lives, and he wants nothing but the best for them. He'll do everything in his power to see that they get that.

So, my brother never knew what it was like to have a positive father figure, yet he's been the best father he can be to his girls by relying on his better judgment when it came to fatherhood. I think this has had both a positive and a negative effect on him as a child and as a man.

The positive effect is that, despite not having a consistent father figure, he didn't let that define the father he would grow to be. In fact, I think it fueled him to be a better father.

The negative effect is that he doesn't have the memories or experiences to share with his daughters of how it felt to be loved and cared for by his own dad. He also can be extremely guarded and protective of certain things in his life, because he never saw how a good father acts or makes decisions.

My brother has a long road ahead of him as a man and father, and he will learn about both. I'm confident he'll overcome not having a positive figure to imitate, and he'll prevail.

My sister and I have basically grown up having a mother/daughter relationship. As her big sister, I cared and provided for her beyond what a sister normally provides. I was the one she looked up to because she didn't spend much time in the care of anyone else, that is until we were forcefully taken from our home. Even then, I had a significant presence in her life whenever and wherever possible. I knew she counted on me to be there for her, so it was my duty at an early age to make sure that I was. This made me very protective of her to the point where it may have been too much.

As she grew into adulthood, I was tough on her, because I didn't want her to make the same mistakes our mother and I had made. I did my best to make sure she was taken care of and that she had better options than the ones my brother and I had growing up. Literally, I would do my best to hurt anyone who messed with my sister.

I knew I was the closest person she had to look up to, so I tried to lead by example, making sure that my choices reflected the best person I could be. She was watching me and often imitated what I did. For this reason, I knew it was vital to create positive and constructive experiences for her that could make a difference in her life, like: finishing high school and going to college; believing in herself and having integrity; becoming independent; chasing her dreams, and more.

This responsibility helped me to make wiser choices as a young adult, big sister, and mother, and presumably prevented a plethora of bad decisions for me. Had I not had the weight on my shoulders of being the role model, provider, and caretaker, it's possible I could have given in to irresponsible choices.

Having obligations influenced my decision-making abilities in a positive way. My responsibilities trained me to think carefully and move cautiously and away from decisions that could take me down a destructive path.

I've always felt it was my civic duty to *lead by example*, not only because of my family responsibilities, but also because I knew that the world badly needs more leaders and good role models. I knew personally what it was like to not have strong parental leadership— and the possible negative outcome from choosing poor role models.

I've learned that you never know who's watching and that you're not just living for yourself. There may be someone we're not aware of who is looking up to us for guidance and inspiration, or counting on us to help make a difference in some way.

It becomes a societal responsibility, in a way, where we must live our lives considering the impact we could have on others, our communities, and the world. Even if we only made a difference in one person's life, that's one more person with hope who could go on to make this world a better place.

I wasn't perfect, but I did my best to teach my sister that there are good and/or bad consequences attached to our choices, so it's important to make wise choices. I did my best to make sure the good choices outweighed the bad. She needed a good example throughout her adolescent years, so that she could grow into the young woman she has become today.

As she took in the good and bad things going on around her, I hoped to create more good memories and examples that would help her. This meant I had to be careful about who I got involved with, and I had to be conscientious about not contradicting the traditional morals and values I was teaching her.

I was careful not to jeopardize my future, preventing me from providing for my loved ones.

These are all of the things I factored into day-to-day living, as I lived my life for my sister, my son, and for me. It was a lot to be responsible for.

It's extremely important, especially when young people are watching and counting on us, that we're diligent and vigilant in our decisions and actions. Young people are more vulnerable and are seeking direction and guidance, primarily from those closest to them. They're easily influenced and need to look to loved ones for affirmation. This is why it's so important that our example has a positive impact on them.

Making decisions that end negatively sets up our youth to make the same mistakes, to be confused about what is actually right. Our poor choices can be the start of a long rocky road of trouble because of what they've learned from watching us. Alternately, seeing positive deeds can set them on the path to do likewise.

My younger sister went everywhere I went when we were growing up. What I did, she did. At one point, I wanted to be a teacher, and she wanted to be one, too. I adored her and knew I was all she had to count on. Because of that, I *had* to succeed. Seeing me succeed would say to her that she could be successful, no matter what obstacles life threw her way.

Our parents loved my sister immensely. However, they weren't in a position to see to it that she had the best chance for a decent future, so I did that. Her well-being and every need was my priority. I wanted to make sure I afforded her all the opportunities she should have as a kid and adolescent. It wasn't always easy to fulfill this role.

Sometimes, I felt I had the weight of the world on my shoulders, with little room for error. Some days I didn't know how I would manage my responsibilities as both a sister and a mother. I wondered why I was the one who had to assume others' responsibilities, since it was hard enough to keep myself grounded and on a straight path.

Although my sister wasn't oblivious to the things going on around her, she didn't understand the magnitude of the consequences of our parents' actions, because I was always there to pick up the pieces and protect her from them—with the exception of the times she was placed in temporary foster care. Oddly, I believe our parents' willingness to be negligent was because they knew I had become that responsible caregiver for my sister and would take care of her while they were irresponsible. I believe they consciously dropped the ball, because I would take care of my sister on their behalf.

As my sister grew into adulthood, I thought I had to be tougher on her and super-critical of her choices. Unfortunately, it has put a wedge between us and we're no longer as close as we once were. Our love for each other is still strong, and I'll always be there for her, but the consistent relationship seems to be gone.

Years ago, I decided to stop wanting more for others than they wanted for themselves, so I fell back and let my sister live her life as she saw fit. I never stopped loving her the same, though.

In hindsight, I may have been carrying a stigma from our past. I was assuming the worst, based on what our parents did. I was afraid to give her too much space, because I didn't want her to take important things lightly. I was reminded every day of the consequences of certain actions and didn't want her to travel that same path.

I no longer wanted to go through what I had gone through because of our parents' substance addictions. I no longer wanted to dedicate my life convincing someone to do better and not use drugs. I did my time, and I didn't want to make any more sacrifices under these circumstances. It wasn't fair. I wasn't the one doing drugs, yet, I suffered their ramifications.

Looking back, I could have done things differently with my sister, such as giving her room to make mistakes and learn from them. It would have been a better approach, and possibly could have kept us close. I automatically assumed the worst at the thought of her sampling drugs, or associating with people in that lifestyle.

I wanted her to be more responsible and, like me, take seriously the planning of her future—going to college and graduate school, starting her own business or building a career for herself, creating financial stability and independence, etc. Because I had taken these things seriously, I expected her to, as well.

I was afraid that, once she started down the wrong path, her life would turn into our parents' life. I lectured her again and again about the importance of not doing drugs and not getting involved with the wrong people, about going to college and building her own brand. It put a wedge between us. Maybe she felt that I was trying to control her life or get her to follow in my footsteps. Maybe she thought I didn't care about the things *she* wanted out of life. I tried the best way I could to guide her and lead by example.

She had the perfect view of what both lifestyles looked like. One involved drugs and substance abuse, and lacked post-high school education and stability. The other did not involve drugs. It included college and a job that afforded stability and growth. I was trying to get her to use the resources we had in front of us for a successful life.

I finally realized that *she* had to want better and do better *for herself.* I couldn't force her into it by lecturing her. She had the best teachers who provided real-life examples. What she did with those examples was a choice *she* had to make, not I. Besides, I had caused myself a lot of stress over my concern for the choices my loved ones made.

It worried me sick, sometimes, trying to get them to make better choices, so that they didn't suffer the consequences of making poor choices. A big lesson I had to learn was this: some things are out of my control and my loved ones will ultimately do what's best for them. Based on that, I had to trust that they *would* make the best decisions.

For reasons unbeknownst to me, I had somehow inherited the role of our family's matriarch. This responsibility was one I took seriously. I had to protect my family and be there for them.

This role didn't come with instructions or how-to manuals. I went according to what I thought was best for us. Living the outcome of others' poor choices has made me extremely guarded and overly protective.

If I noticed my siblings were doing any of the things our parents struggled with, I became extremely concerned. I worried and fussed with them about the implications their actions may have on their life *and mine.* Their actions affected and concerned me just as much as my mother's did, and I was determined that they would not take me down that path again.

I, too, had to be conscientious about what I did. I was no saint and realized it wasn't easy making the right choices—but it was a lot better than making *the wrong ones.* I knew we had to consciously and consistently work on ourselves. It's what I did, and it's what I expected them to do.

I always feared we were bait for that life, because we had grown up accustomed to it. What we saw every day was drugs, alcohol abuse, poverty, and violence, and I desperately did not want us to repeat the cycle. I made it my duty to prevent these things from happening by caring about what my loved ones did and helping them as much as I could.

I tend to react more harshly when it comes to drugs or alcohol abuse than I would anything else. I think about how my mother got involved in these things—being influenced by others. So, I automatically overreact at the thought of my son and my siblings being influenced, as my mother had been. To me, this lifestyle equals being a follower, getting into bad situations that may take a lifetime to get out of.

Whenever I found out that my loved ones were involved in any way with drugs, my natural reaction was usually that the world was coming to an end! I didn't know how to easily deal with anything related to substance abuse. I felt my reaction had to be strong for them to see the bigger picture.

I thought I offered constructive feedback of the harsh reality of their situation. My intentions were never to hurt them, or for them to walk away feeling more wounded than before. I simply tried to prevent a repeat of our past experiences.

My son and my siblings mean the world to me. It was my obligation to show them just that. I acknowledge that I need to work on how I deliver my concerns, and it's something I try to be conscientious about, daily. By nature, showing tough love has been ingrained in me, and it's the only form of support I know how to give. I truly am coming from a genuine place of love and concern.

But I wish that I could be more subtle and less extreme when I'm passionate about something. When it comes to my loved ones, I don't know how to respond with less passion. My motto has always been that I'd rather that they find out about something in the worst way from me, rather than to learn about it in the worst way firsthand.

I'm upset and feel bad when they tell me I've hurt their feelings or gone too far. I often apologize for overreacting. It would hurt me even more if the worst happened and I hadn't said or done anything to prevent it.

My wish is that I didn't have to be guarded and overprotective, but that they would assume personal responsibility, so I could worry less. I don't enjoy doing this—but I also don't want my family to suffer any more than we already have.

It has taken a while for me to realize this—that I have failed if they walk away feeling hurt or attacked. As part of my personal development and growth, I'm understanding that, in some cases, coming off too strong could make matters worse. There are better ways to express concern than to assume the worst. Regardless of what has happened in the past, everyone deserves the benefit of the doubt.

I've also reached the point where I'm not letting others' choices impact my life so significantly. I refuse to live through anyone else's addictions or substance abuse problems as if I'm the one with the addiction. I chose not to put my loved ones through those circumstances, and feel it's not fair that they take me through them.

Everyone should want better *for themselves*. It's not all on me to see that they get it. Constantly worrying and riding them only makes matters worse and drives us further apart. I need more confidence that they'll figure it out and everything will turn out okay in the end.

Besides, I have myself to worry about. I'm still a work in progress, learning as I go. Rome wasn't built in a day, and neither were we. We'll figure this thing out in time and conquer it to the best of our ability.

We don't always get to completely choose our path in life, for I believe it's predestined by a Higher Power. We don't always realize we're carrying the stigma of our past, punishing our loved ones for it. However, when patterns are repeated, the outcome may be the same, or worse. Or it could turn out differently and better.

Everyone is made differently and thinks differently. Some of us learn quicker than others, but that doesn't make them better. It just means they're learning accordingly to the way they know how, and at their own pace. It can't be forced or coerced onto them by someone else.

Some people will have to make their own mistakes to recognize good choices from bad ones. Others learn by *seeing mistakes made by others,* then deciding against making the same choices.

I've learned that what I consider to be a poor choice doesn't mean others see it the same way. We all must reach that point in our lives when *we* want better for ourselves—no one can do it for us.

Key Takeaway from Chapter Seventeen

Shine the light that others might see.

More Takeaways...

- A woman is beautiful not just because of her outward looks, but because of the inward qualities of being independent and ambitious.

- When I had no positive figure in my life to ask for advice, I relied on my own best judgment and common sense, rather than draw from the mistakes I saw being made around me.

- The consequences of others' poor choices and mistakes were my guide for what not to do.

- Early on, I knew that my choices and decisions would influence those around me, especially my little sister.

- I didn't know who was watching, so I made sure my actions were positive and meaningful.

- As a big sister, I led by example so that my choices reflected on the best person I could be.

- Seeking positive role models helps us see things differently, while keeping us from getting derailed or becoming influenced by the negative behaviors we see.

- Seeking advice or guidance from a person who has overcome similar challenges and circumstances is beneficial to our growing into a person who makes better decisions.

- A role model can help us build a brighter future; however, it's up to us to use those opportunities by putting in the necessary work.

- When seeking a positive role model, be aware of who to *not* seek advice from.

- I believe it's my civic duty to *lead by example*, not only because of my responsibilities as a sister and a mother, but also because the world badly needs good leaders and role models.

- In a sense, it's a societal responsibility to consider the impact we could have on others' lives, our communities, and the world.

- Even if you only make a difference in one person's life, that's one more person who has hope, and it's one step closer to making this world a better place.

EIGHTEEN

Insecurities

Growing up without the necessities and financial resources sometimes caused low self-confidence in me—in particular, not feeling pretty because of the poor quality of my clothes. I couldn't afford the cool things to make me look pretty, which basically meant looking like everyone else. I thought I was the most unattractive person.

To be noticed, I thought I had to have the newest trends in clothes, shoes, and accessories. I felt like the guys overlooked me, paying more attention to the "prettier" girls who looked like they came from wealthier backgrounds. I was insecure about how people viewed the "outside" me, rather than letting them get to know the "inside" me.

I recall a time when my mother took my brother and me to a friend's house where she and several girlfriends met. These friends had children, so my brother and I were forced to go outside and play while the adults visited inside. I vividly recall not wanting to go outside, and I especially did not want to be around other kids.

I was ashamed of my worn shoes, afraid the other kids would make fun of me. My shoes had holes at the tops, so I tried hiding them by standing in the corner of the main door with my feet pointed toward the wall. Only my backside and face were visible when I turned to look out at everyone. I was very uncomfortable and humiliated. My feelings were hurt, and I remember feeling bad about it.

I longed to have as much fun as everyone else was having as I heard them scream with laughter. Eventually, I was forced to come out of the corner and join in. They played tag, where I had to put both feet in a circle while one person sang "Eenie, Meenie, Miney, Moe" to determine who was "it." I was so embarrassed and afraid of being looked down on and laughed at because of the condition of my shoes that I just wanted the day to hurry up so we could go home.

As I got older, I had other insecurities about my weight and looks. I didn't wear heels often, nor did I wear makeup. At times, I felt I wasn't as pretty as those who did. Sometimes, the girlfriends I hung out with were, I thought, prettier than me, because I was the last one the boys paid attention to. I thought it was because of my dark skin color, the fact that I didn't wear any makeup, hair extensions, or anything else to enhance my looks. As I matured, I realized that I preferred to be natural. I appreciated not needing to wear makeup, fake nails, hair weaves, and all the rest, to feel beautiful.

I really started to love the skin I was in, and I didn't care if anyone else saw it that way or not. I didn't want to depend on these artifices because I'd have to use them all the time. I wanted to wear a pair of Puma sneakers or Airmax, fitted Khakis or jeans, and feel just as pretty and sexy without overcompensating. These were the standards I lived by.

But, if I decided to switch things up to enhance the beauty I already possessed, it would be for my own reasons and not to look like someone else. I'm not against using beauty or cosmetic products, nor do I knock anyone who uses them regularly. It's simply a personal choice.

As I mature, I've become more open-minded about these things, stepping out of my comfort zone and being more versatile. I'm taking baby steps to find what works best for me.

For my 34th birthday, I wanted to try something different with my hair, and wore extensions for the first time—and loved them! They were fun, convenient, and they saved me a lot of time and stress. I'm also wearing high heels more often. It's been quite challenging, but I enjoy that, as well, though stilettos continue to be a battle for me. I'm sure I'll venture out more if and when I decide to.

The fact is, I've embraced who I am. Learning that beauty begins on the inside, I've become more at ease and more contented with myself. It seems to have had an effect on others and caused them to see the beauty I possess, inside and out. I realize that it's okay to be different, as long as I'm humbly confident with myself, and I'm no longer changing something because I lack self-esteem.

My battle with insecurity taught me that if you feel good on the inside, you look just as good on the outside. There's no rule or science to what is and isn't beauty. It's all about interpretation and confidence. Growing up with less only made me appreciate the things that I do have. Not being able to afford the latest fashion trends didn't take away from who I was or the person I was destined to become. In fact, doing without those things motivated me to work harder for what I wanted, and to be more compassionate toward those also living without.

In some ways, growing up poor humbled me. The important things in life aren't material things; they're more about character and tenacity. I lived to wake up each morning and managed to get myself to and from school in those holey shoes and worn-out clothes. I aspired to be someone when I grew up in those hand-me-down garments. And when I was blessed with new clothes and shoes, even if they were secondhand, I appreciated them and took care of them like they were my last.

Having less than others also taught me the value in being satisfied with what I *could* afford; to not let greed or lust cause me to miss out on the more important things in life.

As I grew into young womanhood, I learned that the clothes I wore didn't **define** my destiny or my beauty. And I realized that I didn't **need** all of the things everyone else had. However, if I **wanted** a certain style, then I had to work hard to afford it and maintain it.

I'm thankful for the hardships we experienced, because they allowed me to adapt to various conditions and to persevere. I can go from rags to riches or from riches to rags and still be happy and content. It isn't always easy to remain humble, but when I reflect on where I've come from, it puts things in perspective.

Key Takeaway from Chapter Eighteen

Exude confidence by doing what feels good.

More Takeaways...

- As I came of age, I became more content with myself and appreciated how I didn't need to look like everyone else to feel beautiful.

- I started to love the skin I was in and didn't care if anyone else saw me that way.

- I didn't want to depend on beauty aids to make me feel pretty, because then I would have to use them all the time.

- Learning that beauty starts within, I became more comfortable and content with myself.

- If I decide to enhance the beauty I already possess, it will be for my own reasons and not to look like someone else or because I lack self-esteem.

- Growing up with less only made me better appreciate what I do have.

- I couldn't afford the latest fashion trends, but that didn't take away from who I was or the person I was to become.

- Doing without motivated me to work harder for what I wanted, and to be more compassionate toward those also living without.

- I woke up each morning and got myself to and from school in holey shoes and worn-out clothes.

- Wearing those hand-me-downs helped me aspire to become someone.

- When I was blessed with new clothes and shoes, even if they were secondhand, I appreciated them and took care of them as if they were my last.

- Growing up with less has taught me the importance of working hard to afford and maintain the things I want and need.

NINETEEN

The Fallacy of Love

We look for love for many reasons—to fill a void, to mask pain, and because it's normal and necessary for a happy life. Whatever the reason, we feel we must have another person's love, and we're willing to go through great lengths to find it.

Growing up, I had an insatiable hunger for love. It's hard to know which type I longed for and wasn't getting enough of, but I thought it was in the form of a relationship with a man.

I looked forward to being loved and deeply cared about by someone who made me feel happy and secure.

I had always been enamored by older men, men I could look up to. I was attracted to their maturity and wisdom. Coincidentally, most men I was drawn to happened to be older. It's not that I was opposed to dating someone my own age, however.

Now that I look back, I'm not sure I was looking for love for the right reasons. I had never gotten it from the one man who should have given it to me unconditionally and endlessly, my father. I never knew what it felt like to be loved by a doting father.

In our society, I hear the concerns about boys growing up without a father, but I think it's just as critical for girls. We need it just as much, so that we don't look for a father's love from other men—or people, in general—potentially making us vulnerable and at risk to be hurt or taken advantage of.

I used to fantasize about being with my father, doing fun things with him, hearing him say sweet things to me, hugging me.

I wanted my daddy. Seeing other girls with their fathers was always painful while I was growing up—and still is to this day. Watching fathers and their daughters on television has always been a sore spot, and made me extremely sad and wishful. I dreamt about feeling the comfort of my father's arms around me and holding me tight.

One of the songs Beyoncé sings is a tribute to her father. Such beautiful lyrics—who would have thought they could be so painful to hear. I would torture myself listening to the song, over and over. I was living vicariously through that song.

In some past relationships, I became extra needy for the man's love and affection. I needed to feel loved far beyond companionship, to feel secure, like I really mattered.

I realize now that I put unfair pressure on the men I've dated by setting my expectations too high.

I expected them to make up for what I didn't get growing up. Instead of focusing on ways to make the man-woman relationship stronger, I looked for a nurturing, parental figure to make me feel content.

Early in my relationship with my son's father, things were great. I was really into him because he brought laughter and peace into a life of problems. I thought our relationship would continue this way and that we would be together for a long time.

Because of all the drama going on in my life, I was skeptical that anyone would want to date or love me. But he didn't judge me at all. In fact, he and my mom became really close. She liked him, and he always made her laugh. She loved him like a son and appreciated the man he was to me. As our relationship grew, I invested more trust in him and was more open.

He came from a happy family where he was raised by both parents—quite the opposite of mine. I was intimidated at first, expecting that his family would judge or scrutinize me because of my upbringing and the issues I was still having at home. But they didn't.

At first, I didn't think my son's father was capable of hurting me, considering the bond we had formed. He was truly one of my greatest friends at the time.

Unfortunately, that was short-lived and changed when he betrayed me by being unfaithful. I learned of his infidelities while I was pregnant with our son. I was devastated, extremely disappointed, and I remember my shock and disbelief when I found out. It was a very painful experience.

The hurt, the deceit, the disappointment—it all felt like I had been in this place before. Up to that point, he had never given me a reason for not trusting him and I believed everything he said.

That feeling of happiness, peace, and serenity when we began dating was suddenly gone. It was so far gone that I knew the next lie, hurt, and disappointment was right around the corner. I had been a believer, at first, but, after that incident, I knew things could never be the same between us. Even so, I still wanted my son to be raised in a drug-free home, so I eventually forgave him and got back with him.

Slowly, my part in the relationship changed. Things weren't the same anymore, and I began distancing myself. All I cared about was making *me* happy. Although we lived together with our son, I was emotionally absent. I partied without him, I hung out with friends, came home late, dated other guys—you name it. I wasn't the same person he had met in January 1994. The tables had turned, now it was him who was stressed out about how things were. Beyond my responsibilities as a mother and sister, I didn't have a care in the world. And he could never correct or undo the pain he had caused me.

Psychologically, I was in a place where I didn't care or think about how I may have been mistreating him. I was so ready to leave him, but I was still in high school and didn't have anywhere else to go. I stuck it out, but remained emotionally unavailable to love him.

Around the time I graduated high school, my mom got situated, and I went to live with her while I looked for a place of my own.

After moving on from my son's father, I decided to give another try at loving someone. I fell in love with a man whom I thought I could spend the rest of my life with. Unfortunately, he lived a life-style that prevented that from ever happening. We had grown up in similar backgrounds—living in poverty with drug-addicted parents—but we had each chosen a different path.

His way of prospering was different from mine. I went to school and got a corporate job, while he chose the streets. He was very quiet and, outside of his close friends, kept to himself. He was a person liked by some, but feared by most. He had money and power, which I was attracted to. He had status and made a name for himself. He wasn't seen or heard when it came to his business in the streets.

Aside from his street credibility, he was a kind and sweet person who anyone's mother and grandmother could adore. He was soft inside and had a weak spot for me. I could get away with anything and he'd love me the same. He was genuine and truly had my back.

We dated on and off since I was 12 years old until we were young adults. He was one of my brother's closest friends. When he came to our house to visit my brother, I would always meddle with him and call him mean names. That was my way of showing that I liked him. He patiently waited for me to grow up, to see how much he really cared and wanted to be with me.

We got back together after I broke up with my son's father. By then, I was head over heels in love with him. He was my first true love and life was wonderful. It had taken years to finally get to this place of love, only to learn that our vastly different lifestyles would bring it to an end.

I thought I could love him and be with him without being a part of his other world, but I quickly learned that it wasn't possible to separate the two. Although I loved him unconditionally, living such a lifestyle was not what I wanted for my son and me. But I did want some of the qualities I liked and admired about him—success, power, influence, stability, and tenacity—but I wanted it the right way, morally.

Although I enjoyed being spoiled with lavish gifts and getting whatever I wanted, I didn't want to risk my life for it. Besides, my conscience wouldn't allow me to support this lifestyle, knowing how morally wrong it was and how it damages families. We talked about him changing his lifestyle.

Change didn't come soon enough.

He was arrested and sentenced to 17 years in prison. It was a wake-up call for me, and a reality check that I was not about that life. In the beginning of his prison sentence, we kept in touch, but then we both moved on. He will always be special to me.

■ ■ ■

I'm pretty laid back in my relationships and try not to sweat the small stuff. I'm an equal opportunist and believe that loyalty and devotion go both ways. If I'm making an effort and sacrifice to remain as a couple, so should my partner. To me, it's just practical.

But it hasn't always been the case for me. Therefore, if it isn't working, I may choose to end a relationship right away. It usually turns out that the decision to end the relationship is best for both of us. Why waste precious time on something we feel isn't going to grow?

It's not always easy to walk away, though. My approach in overcoming a failed relationship is, if I could overcome the letdown and disappointment caused by two of the most important people in my life, my parents, then it should be easier to overcome a failed relationship. Thinking this way works for me. That doesn't make me mean, cold-hearted, or emotionless; it's just my way of coping with hurt and disappointment. Up front, I give everyone the benefit of the doubt.

I'm generally very optimistic and hopeful when it comes to

growing into a relationship. When hope and trust fade, it's almost impossible for me to remain enthusiastic and optimistic for a future together. Though some may look at this as my being unforgiving or selfish, that's just not the way it is.

After a while, finding love and companionship stopped being a priority; raising my son, completing college, and building my career *were* priorities. I felt that a serious relationship and commitment could distract or deter me, so I put them on the back burner for the time being.

My son was the number one man in my life, and I didn't want to share that space with anyone. Occasionally, I dated for companionship, but nothing major. I just wasn't interested. The most attractive thing to me growing up was success and forward movement. I didn't want to lose sight of those things, so I mostly kept everyone I dated at a distance.

Some of my close friends and family members think that my upbringing has hardened me and is partly why I haven't fallen in love yet. They also feel that my standards and expectations for my ideal man or husband are either too high or unrealistic. Some feel I'm too strong-willed and void of emotions. Basically, they don't think I'm capable of opening up enough to love or let anyone in.

I would agree that some of my past experiences play a part in my ambition, willpower, and determination to succeed. What they don't know and fail to realize is that, quite contrary to what they believe, my past does not influence my willingness to love.

What people see is me staying disciplined and focused on my goals and minimizing any distractions that could take me off course. I admit to being strong-willed (when necessary) while protecting my heart and not being blinded by love. Any lack of emotion may just be me not being into the man I'm dating.

These are defense mechanisms I've developed to guide me in falling in love with the right man and preventing me from settling for just anyone. Until it happens, my mission is to keep working toward my goals.

It's unfortunate that my philosophy on relationships is often misconstrued and taken out of context. I'm a hopeless romantic when it comes to finding true love. When I finally do meet my one true love, I intend to love hard and unconditionally. Although it may not come easy for me, I don't doubt that it will happen.

Prior relationships taught me that compatibility is key to my happiness and fulfillment. I long for the man who shares similar qualities, such as religion, honesty, success, ambition, drive, and someone who is family-oriented. But I also want someone who, together, can make one another greater. I strongly believe in these things, and I refuse to compromise or settle.

Besides, I wanted to put all my focus on being a mother, completing school, and securing my future, all challenges in themselves, but my top priorities. Adding a relationship at that point would have complicated things even further.

I believe that, to have a successful relationship, you must have a strong foundation. I didn't want to add to the stress of securing a better future with the day-to-day challenges of keeping up a strong and healthy relationship. Now that I'm in a good place—completed undergraduate and graduate studies, worked for over 14 years in my career—I'm ready for the next chapter in my life by experiencing true love with a life partner.

In far too many relationships, people have an underlying purpose, other than sharing love and companionship with their partner. Some are looking for a cure-all for problems they can't fix or cope with on their own. Those who are in these situations may not be aware that these reasons may put additional strain on a relationship and bring on epic failure.

To ensure a person is not in a relationship for the wrong reasons, we should know what we want from the other person. Knowing this ahead of time can increase the chances for a healthy, successful relationship.

If we're determined not to bring our past experiences into our present relationship, we increase our chances for success. If we feel we're lacking something important in our lives, perhaps that's the time to seek help before getting serious with someone.

My takeaway from past relationships is that it's okay to build walls to minimize the chances of becoming vulnerable or being hurt, but the walls shouldn't be so high that no one can climb over them.

I've also realized that some things are just inevitable in life and out of my control. What's most important is resilience and effective damage control.

Key Takeaway from Chapter Nineteen

Fix old problems to prevent creating new ones.

More Takeaways...

- It's equally important for girls as it is for boys to have a positive father figure in their lives.

- As a young adult, I realized that not having my father in my life as a child and youth impacted my relationships with others.

- Addressing or resolving issues from the past increases chances for successful relationships in the future.

- I had to be aware of not allowing scars from my past to affect my future relationships.

- Unaware, I had set too-high expectations for my relationships, trying to compensate for what I had lacked from my relationships with my father and stepfather.

- I had to prioritize between building a romantic relationship and building a future for my son and for me.

- Achieving my goals was pivotal to being successful as a partner; therefore, early on, I sacrificed finding love so I could focus on my son, completing my education, and building a career.

- I learned from past relationships that it's okay to build walls whenever necessary; just not so high where no one can climb over them.

- Some things are simply inevitable and outside our control.

- Resilience and effectively applying damage control is most important in relationships.

TWENTY

Some Things Are Just Not Good Enough

My mother's personality changed, depending on her mood. For instance, when she was clean for a long period of time due to recovery, she was a fun and loving person to be around. When she was clean by circumstance—no money to buy drugs—she could go from 0 to 10 in a second. She would be short-tempered, on edge, and she could get mean and nasty, at times.

At first, I gave in to her rants and raves, just to keep the peace. I fell for the lies she told me about why she needed money, that it was for food, bus fare, or to pay a bill, and I would give it to her out of pity. When I got tired of the lies and giving her my hard-earned money to supply her habits, she became extremely mean and nasty. Sometimes, she acted a complete fool and tried bullying us into giving in to her rants and raves.

It infuriated me when she behaved like this. I got tough and stern and wouldn't tolerate it. In time, I stopped giving in to her demands when she couldn't find a way to get high. Depending on the circumstances, I politely saw her to the door, or I left.

As I stood my ground and told her *"NO,"* I gave back the same energy she gave me. This often made it awkward and uncomfortable afterwards, because what had started out as a good time became tainted by her fixation on getting high.

Times like these prevented her from providing unconditional love and support as a mother. Her urge to get high and frustration at not having the funds to do so made it difficult for her to think about anyone else's needs but her own. Because of it, she and I missed out on mother/daughter moments that I wish we'd had.

One example is when I told her I was buying my first home. She reacted the complete opposite of what I expected or hoped for. I thought she would say she was proud of such a huge accomplishment and proud of me.

Boy, I had never been more overly optimistic! Her reaction was everything *but* that!

We were in the car when I told her the news. She acted as if I was some random person that she was jealous of and we ended up arguing. All I can remember is speeding up so we would get to her destination sooner. Her reaction was disappointing and took the joy out of my good news.

I couldn't believe she wasn't happy for me. I expected her, of all people, to be happy and supportive. I thought that was what mothers were supposed to be, regardless of their own circumstances. I was expecting unconditional, genuine love and support. I was hoping I had made her even more proud of me with such an accomplishment. She knew how hard I had worked to provide a better life for my son and me. She also knew how much I had given of myself to help our family, and the sacrifices I had made.

For once it was about me, it was finally my moment, and she was too selfish to celebrate it with me. I was hurt and exasperated. It was the worst feeling in the world. I could never imagine being this way with my son. Somehow, I was supposed to not let this affect me or steal my joy. That was tough.

My mom's reaction made me apprehensive about being so elated and sharing my news with others. If the one person who should have been the proudest turned out to be the most unsupportive, then why should I expect others to be happy for me? So much for thinking I had done something right that would make my mother as happy as I was.

As I grew into adolescence and young adulthood, my relationship with my mother was strained, for the most part. My brother was more like her best friend, my sister was her baby, and I was stuck somewhere in the middle. I never felt like my mother had a connection with me, as she had had with my siblings. Ours seemed forced. It was probably due to my disdain for her lifestyle, the choices she made, and my refusal to accept them. I expected more from her and would never be okay with her getting high.

My disapproval was consistent and unwavering, whereas my sister and brother were more tolerant and forgiving. On rare occasions, she made me feel like I was loved by her and just as special to her as my siblings. I treasured those times and tried to hang onto them as long as I could, because I didn't know when they would come again.

When I was in foster care, I envisioned how I planned to make my mother laugh the next time I was allowed to visit with her. I fantasized about making her happy and me feeling like I meant the world to her. I really wanted to feel like I mattered more than any drug or addiction. I believe she held it against me for having higher expectations of her as a mother and woman.

Those few times I talked to my mother about things that had happened to us, she denied them or got very upset about them. She would say that they weren't true, or insinuate that the past is the past.

I found it interesting when she denied what took place, because I wished those things had been fictitious, too—but they weren't! It just wasn't cool that she was in denial or flat out couldn't remember these things. It made me angry with her, the fact that *she* had inflicted this pain on us and *conveniently* chose not to remember any of it. She neither acknowledged that she had made our lives a living hell, nor was she accountable about where she went wrong, and she didn't apologize for it. She didn't care to offer any explanations as to why it happened. It made me furious, and I resented her even more.

I just wanted to talk about some of the things that went on in my life over the years, in hopes of finally releasing the bad memories that had haunted me for so long. I thought it would help to release some of the pain and frustration I held onto and for which I blamed her.

I needed to hear her explain why these things happened. I needed her to apologize for allowing them to take place. I guess I felt that an explanation and apology would make me feel better. I looked for affirmation that she loved me and that none of those things would have happened had her life turned out differently. Unfortunately, that never happened.

She never talked about any wrongdoing on her part, or asked how we felt. She never asked if anything had happened to us, or if we were hurting in any way because of it. It's like she either didn't want to face the truth, or she didn't care enough. It made me angry and left me feeling like she only cared about herself.

I didn't understand how she could move through life without being either concerned or curious whether we were okay while she wasn't there for us. I didn't understand how she didn't want to know if anyone had ever hurt me, or if I was ever afraid. For me, as a mother, these are things I would have needed to know first, so that I could reassure my children that they were now okay, and that I would always protect them going forward.

I guess she didn't feel that way; or, perhaps, she simply couldn't commit to preventing those situations from happening again. It just made me sad to know that she didn't care enough to find out if something was wrong, or to apologize and give me the secure feeling that I didn't have to worry about those things ever again.

Key Takeaway from Chapter Twenty

Believe in yourself.

More Takeaways...

- My happiness and success are not measured by validation or acclaim from others.

- I learned not to seek approval from others to validate my success.

- Believing in myself was the greatest reward and recognition I needed.

- Be proud of your accomplishments, regardless of whether others are.

- I stood my ground and did not give in to the pressure and demands of supporting others' addictions and bad habits.

TWENTY-ONE

Lessons My Mom Taught Me

As I got older, I learned about my mother's growing-up years. Allegedly, my grandfather was extremely abusive to my maternal grandmother, his first wife, and to his second wife, as well. I also learned that he was abusive to his children, and very mean, at times.

Of my mom's four siblings, I only grew up close to two of them. They didn't talk much about their childhood, at least not to us, but when they did, it usually wasn't positive. I cannot recall one good memory or story they shared with us about their childhood. It doesn't mean there weren't any, but it sounded like there weren't many.

Perhaps my mom's childhood is why we're left with so many unanswered questions about her inability to be a nurturing mother. Maybe she loved us the way she was treated growing up.

My mother was very matter-of-fact and explicit when teaching us valuable lessons. She was stern as she articulated the consequences of good and bad choices. In fact, she was a living example of both.

When it came to disciplining us as consequences for our poor choices as children, she didn't hold back any punches. She resorted to what she believed to be suitable disciplinary actions for our misbehavior, mostly whippings and tongue-lashings. This was her way of instilling good morals, values, and beliefs. This was her attempt to prevent us from repeating the same mistake or bad decision. I appreciate her for that, because, for the most part, those lessons stuck with us.

I believe her punishments and disciplinary actions helped keep us from going down a path of perpetual bad behavior that could have caused us to be worse off. I appreciate her telling me the raw facts of being an adolescent parent, and that the odds of me having a successful future and living the "American Dream" as a 15-year-old mother were slim to none.

She also taught me that, to beat the odds, I had to set goals and come up with a plan for achieving them.

I'm pretty sure my brother would say that he appreciated her being upfront and direct with him when he was being a knucklehead out in the streets. She basically told him that if and when he went to jail, she wasn't getting him out.

Overall, she helped us to identify which side we were going to be on, the good or the bad—despite how *her shortcomings affected our lives*. She didn't want us using that as an excuse for making poor choices or following in her footsteps.

The most important lesson she taught us as children was that, to get through anything in life, we needed to have the Most Powerful Resource with us every step of the way.

She made sure we had a connection with God, and that we knew how to talk to Him through prayer. I imagine this is the way she could get through life without her mother by her side. She did have her sister and stepmother, but there is nothing like having unconditional love and comfort from your natural mother.

I believe I get my tough skin from my mother. She was a rebel at times, and feisty. I recall being chased home from the park by a group of kids. I ran like my life depended on it. As I got closer to home, I was screaming, fear in my voice, for my mom. She hurried down the stairs with my brother following. Once I got to her, I held her and cried. I felt safe. She was so upset by the state of panic I was in that she told me to never run from kids again, and if there was a next time, to pick up something and knock them out with it.

Looking back, I believe her meaning wasn't about the *physical aspect* of the fight; she was adamant about the *principle* of facing my fear and not running from it. Basically, take it by storm and conquer it.

That very lesson has stayed with me—that life is full of unexpected challenges, and the best thing to do is to face them head on.

I think back to that fight whenever I face tough challenges. It gives me courage and strength to overcome any obstacles. It was on that day that my mommy taught me to stand up for myself, no matter how impossible the task may seem. Not only did this lesson give me mental and physical strength and courage, but it's also given me the armor I need to get through the difficulties I've experienced.

I'm able to be strong-willed when I need to be. It's the seemingly small things like this that have made such a substantial impact on my life, allowing me to appreciate the woman my mother was to me.

Because of her, I'm braver and stronger than I ever thought I could be. In a way, her strength and courage have made me want to be just like her. She wasn't afraid to try, and she never gave up without a fight.

Key Takeaway from Chapter Twenty-One

Not everything has to be a fight.

More Takeaways...

- Everything isn't always black and white in parenting or displaying affection.

- People do things based on what they know and what they've experienced.

- Life is full of unexpected challenges, so manage them by facing them head on.

- Be emotionally aware of the energy you project to others while standing up for something you feel passionate about.

- Pick your battles wisely; not every battle requires you to be defensive.

TWENTY-TWO

This Wasn't Supposed To Happen

t was December of 2006. I hosted a Christmas dinner at my home for my family and friends. My mother was among those who attended. When the evening ended, she stayed behind so that we could talk.

That night, she told me she had been diagnosed with Stage IV lung cancer, meaning it was terminal. I was shocked and didn't know how to react. I couldn't fully process this news, so I immediately urged her to stay with my son and me.

While she lived with us, I noticed the same pattern developing as when my dad had lived with me for a short time. I didn't feel at ease. It was difficult to sit with her as if things were normal. I felt bad and didn't understand why I was so uncomfortable being around my own mother. As I had done when my dad lived with us, I mainly stayed up in my room. Like my father, she, too, told my brother that she felt unwelcome and all alone. I didn't do it intentionally or consciously; it was just a natural reaction. If there was anyone I would rather be around, it was definitely my mom, but I just didn't know how.

There was so much I wanted to talk to her about. I thought it would be a great opportunity for us to mend our differences, and I could finally overcome the disdain I felt toward her, feelings I had harbored for several years. I wanted to share with her all the moments when I was hurt and afraid and felt alone. I wanted to hear her say "I'm sorry" and tell me she loved me. I wanted her to tell me that, if it hadn't been for the drugs, none of those things would have ever happened.

Unfortunately, that didn't happen. She didn't seem open to talking about the past, nor was she interested in knowing how we survived such difficult times without her. She also never accepted the fact that she was going to die from her illness; she was in denial. In fact, talking about death upset her.

Although she still had a decent quality of life at this point, she battled drug addiction and she smoked cigarettes. No matter how critical her situation was, I wouldn't allow her to do either in my home. If she wanted to smoke a cigarette, she had to go outside. When she had an opportunity to get high, she went elsewhere.

I pleaded with her to stop, but to no avail. She did both until she wasn't physically able to anymore.

Even though my mother was terminally ill, I wouldn't lower my expectations of her. I held her to the same high expectations as before. I was not going to excuse her drug habits because of her condition.

My brother and sister, on the other hand, mainly my brother, were more lenient. My brother once suggested that I let her do the things she wanted to do since she only had a short time to live. I told him that she could move in with him and he could let her, but I would not allow it. They loved her just as much as I did, but we had differing viewpoints on certain things.

As my mother's health deteriorated, it became difficult for me to care for her on my own, so I put her into hospice to get proper care for her. It was a tough decision, and it hurt me the day we took her and I had to leave without her. She didn't want to be there and begged to come back home with me. This really affected me mentally and emotionally.

It felt like the same sorrow I had when we dropped my sister off at daycare, and how she would cry uncontrollably for us not to leave her. Every time, it had me in tears, and weighed heavily on my mind until we returned to get her.

It's exactly how I felt each night, leaving my mother in the hospice facility. It bothered me so much because I could relate to being forced to separate from a loved one, not knowing when you would see him or her again. It was extremely hard to let go.

Less than two weeks after putting my mother into hospice, I vividly recall the day the hospice nurse called to inform me that my mother's vitals were dropping. I rushed down to the hospital. She had been taken to a temporary holding area where terminally ill patients go before being assigned to ICU. My mother and I were alone with several physicians.

I held her hand and looked into her eyes and noticed tears as I spoke to her. She wasn't responsive, but the tears let me know she was coherent enough to know that I was there.

More family showed up. We were taken to a family room until they got her situated in ICU.

In the meantime, I decided to pick up my son from the neighbor's and take him to his father's or grandparents' house.

While I was on my way, my aunt called and told me that I needed to come back to the hospital right away. "Is there anything wrong," I kept asking, but she would only say that I should come right back.

By the time I got there, my mother had been moved to a different wing of the hospital. I walked into her room and saw my brother crying. I don't know how or why, but I asked him what was wrong, why wasn't she responding? He acted surprised that I could ask such a question. I vividly recall him saying, "What do you *think* is wrong?! She's dead!" I couldn't fully process what he'd just said. I was in utter shock. There were no sounds in the room for what seemed like an eternity. Nothing was making any sense to me.

At first, I didn't feel anything, and I didn't want to cry. Then I forced myself to cry, because I thought it was the right thing to do and because everyone was looking at me for a reaction.

I sat, disbelieving, in a chair alongside her bed, still in utter shock. I hadn't been gone that long, how could this have happened?

I'd been there all morning with her, and it seemed like she would be with us for a bit longer.

Part of me felt like the life I'd always imagined having with her had yet to begin. How could she leave before we got to that point? We were just getting on the right track for that to happen. She was with me in a different way, different from all the other times, she was no longer getting high, even if it was because she was too sick, it was still signs of the life… the life of having our sober, loving mommy who was going to always be there from here on out to protect us. The mommy I went to bed knowing would be there when I woke up in the morning.

I didn't want to accept that it was over and that I would never get the mommy I had always yearned for. This had been the one thing I had missed out on all my life, the root of all my problems, and the only resolution to fixing them… and now, it would never be.

After a couple of hours, I went home. I went straight upstairs to my room and laid across the bed for what seemed like hours, staring at the ceiling as people came in to check on me.

Later that night, when I was alone, I went downstairs to my mother's room and collapsed on the middle of the floor.

I was overcome with sorrow, grief, and fear. It was by far the worst feeling I had ever experienced. I cried uncontrollably next to my mother's bed as I clutched the nightgown she had last worn. I felt so alone, so terrified. I so badly wanted my sister and brother at that moment, but they were at home with their loved ones. I kept thinking how this wasn't fair. I wanted my mommy back in her bed at that very moment, and it didn't happen. I needed her then like I had never needed her before. I would have given anything to hear her voice and smell her scent. It just didn't seem fair.

Oddly, now that I no longer have my mother, I'm baffled that, for a lifetime, I felt like I didn't have a mom. I complained about her not being the mother I needed her to be, I complained that she wasn't providing me with enough love and affection. Today, I would give anything just to have even that much from her.

I miss her so much. Part of my soul feels empty.

Right after she passed, I hoped and wished that I would find a letter addressed to me, telling me all the things I wanted her to say while she was still here. I wanted to read her true thoughts and feelings on how much she loved me and was proud of me.

Sometimes, there are moments that remind me of her, especially when I'm around my siblings, and I miss her even more.

My longing for her intensifies when I'm in certain places, and then I'll be overwhelmed with sorrow. It's a paralyzing feeling that sometimes leaves me weeping uncontrollably.

I would give anything to have her back, and, this time, it would be different. This time, I would try my best to accept her for who she is and all that comes with it. This time, I would do my best to look past the things she didn't do, and focus on the present.

There's just so much I still need her for. It's like a hole of happiness that has been permanently burned out of my life, and I'm unable to replace it. I'm hoping that, in time, I'll fill that void with the happy memories I do have of my mother, and be content with them.

Key Takeaway from Chapter Twenty-Two

Live in or take advantage of the present.

More Takeaways...

- I wish I had taken advantage of the opportunity to talk with my mother about the things I had harbored that bothered me.

- Losing a loved one has taught me the importance of taking advantage of the moment, so that you're not living with regrets or wishing you had done things differently.

- In hindsight, I wish I had relished the good and bad moments while my mother was still alive.

- In hindsight, I wish I had accepted what I couldn't change or what I had no control over to get past things my mother did not do, so I could embrace my love for her even more.

- Early on, address issues and differences with your loved ones, so that you move forward quicker and spend less time apart.

TWENTY-THREE

Having Something To Believe In

Through all the turmoil in our lives, our mother managed to instill a religious belief in us, and made going to church a regular part of our lives. Regardless of what had happened the night before, or what our current state of affairs looked like, my mother was determined for us to go to church.

During these times, I gained comfort in believing in a higher power who was watching out for us, and who I could talk to with my head bowed and my eyes closed. I could tell this person or spirit all the things I felt, and ask for help. Most of the time, I felt this person was listening, and my requests were answered. This gave me hope and helped me believe that the things they said about God and Christianity were true.

Due to my belief and faith in God and the Holy Spirit, I didn't feel alone, in a sense. When things got bad when I was a child, I'd pray that God or the Holy Spirit would make things better for us. At some point and in some fashion, things did work out, or the storm would finally end. Although storms did reoccur, I reached a comfort level that, when I closed my eyes and prayed, we would get through it. This continued into my adulthood, as my faith strengthened and increased.

As the dynamics of my life changed, the storms came more frequently and the problems I faced were different. The one thing that remained constant was my ability to rely on what I believed in and in my faith.

My pastor at True Vine Missionary Baptist Church of Minnesota once said that, *if you don't stand for something, you'll fall for anything.* It's a statement that has always resonated with me, for some reason. When I first heard it, I right away thought it was meant for me. I thought it meant I could choose to follow in the footsteps of my past, or I could choose to stand up to it and take a different route.

People living a significant amount of their lives in toxic environments usually end up repeating what they're most familiar with; especially when the majority of the people around them do the same thing. It's challenging to be different and believe there is a better way. It has to become a cause you truly believe in and will fight for, even if you are the only one fighting.

For me, that cause was to not repeat the sins of my past, or what my parents and community did. I challenged myself to think and make different choices. I didn't want to be poor or addicted to drugs or alcohol. I didn't want to live where resources were scarce.

I wanted a better life, and getting it meant I had to think differently than the others around me. To me, this meant doing well in school and studying for every test or exam, keeping up with my homework and staying focused at school, creating goals for my future and working diligently to accomplish them. I knew that it was going to be a lot of work, but I had no other choice if I wanted something better. My trust and belief in God is the reason I'm still fighting for my cause.

I didn't stand a chance against the poverty, violence, and drug wars that plagued the environment I grew up in. It was my faith in God that I would be delivered unto better times and conditions without latching onto what went on around me.

It was my faith and belief that kept me from conforming to the toxic environment I lived in every day of my life while growing up; enduring terrible times, inhaling the toxic drugs that filled the air under the same roof where I lived.

All of the calamities around me did not break me or lure me into that world. I felt I'd been chosen to withstand it and come out even better, based on my spiritual belief and faith in God.

My mom once told me that I was a "chosen one," and for a long time, I didn't know what she had meant. Initially, I thought, *why would someone want to be chosen for such a tumultuous lifestyle*; what was God thinking when He picked me? But, as I grew spiritually, I figured out what she had meant.

Not everyone could sustain such an upbringing and keep their head on straight. Statistics show that the majority end up becoming a product of their environment and repeating the same vicious cycle. For some reason, I was different. I often wondered if God had a different plan for me, and that, perhaps, He wanted to use me as a testimony to others. Maybe He wanted me to demonstrate that the best weapons one can have in their arsenal are faith and hope.

No matter how bad or painful the situation became, I prayed for God to help us through it. Each time, *He* did help. It may not have been how we wanted, and we may have suffered some bruises mentally and physically, but *He* always brought us through it.

This is why I've always believed that the sky is the limit, and that nothing was impossible for me to accomplish. There were plenty of times I wanted to give up and give into sorrow or pressure, but, spiritually, I've always found a way out of that state of mind.

Something always came along to console me that my struggles had a meaningful purpose. This understanding helped fuel my motivation and encouraged me to keep pushing forward.

Being connected with God showed me a clear path to a brighter future, even when our lights were out and when we were left home alone with no food to eat. I could still see and understand what I had to do to ensure that this didn't continue to happen to my family and me.

In the end, *faith is what kept hope alive* for me, as well as for my mother. She, too, had a strong faith. I watched her pray and praise

Him through good and bad times, and I've witnessed the miracles that *He* bestowed on us.

I instilled the same religious beliefs in my son. Even though I'm his mother and have his best interests at heart, I'm human with imperfections. I want him to know that, by putting his faith in God, he'll never be misguided, even if I fail him.

Now I know my Pastor's meaning when he said if we don't stand for something we'll fall for anything. I stand for my Christian beliefs, which have been my source of strength every day of my life while on this journey.

My advice is that, if you believe in a higher power, study and see how it can help you in your journey. Truly believing in something can make a huge difference. You'll make better choices and become a better person overall.

Whatever you believe in, learn about it and find the good that will make life better for you and others.

Key Takeaway from Chapter Twenty-Three

Believe in something or fall for anything.

More Takeaways...

- Having faith in a higher power gave me hope and encouragement through tough times, in my family home and in my own, as I embarked on my journey to success.

- Throughout the years, what remained constant was my ability to rely on my faith and what I believed in.

- Overcoming adversity has to become a cause that you truly believe in and will fight for, even if you're the only one.

- My cause was to not repeat the sins of my past or the decisions of my parents and community.

- I knew I did not want to be poor or to become addicted to drugs or alcohol.

- I didn't want to live where resources were scarce and limited.

- I challenged myself to think differently and make different choices. These included, but were not limited to:

  - Doing well in school and studying for every test or exam.

  - Keeping up with my homework and staying focused at school.

  - Creating goals for my future and working diligently to accomplish them.

- I knew it would be a lot of work, but I had no other choice if I wanted to stand for a better cause.

- My trust and belief in God is the reason I am still standing and fighting for my cause.

- I felt I was chosen to come out on top, based on my spiritual belief and faith in God.

- Whatever you believe, learn about it and find the good in it that will allow you to apply it to make life better for you and others.

TWENTY-FOUR

Determination and Willpower

Most people would agree that life isn't easy. While this popular cliché holds merit for some, it isn't the case for everyone. Some firmly believe that life is what you make it, but that it may be harder for others. Being raised in poverty may be a challenge, but the same holds true for those who come from better home environments; they just have different struggles. Growing up with scarcity can serve to motivate a person to succeed at beating the odds.

Overcoming challenges and struggles is generally a choice. What you put into it is what you get out of it. Deciding to step out from under a life of poverty and into a life of opportunity and prosperity is possible with hard work and determination. In my opinion, we're not born with determination and willpower; we acquire it.

From early on, I loved getting ahead, and I loved school. Working hard and not giving up easily came naturally for me. I loved taking on challenges when I was least expected to succeed. I thrived at excelling and exceeding all expectations, all the while trying to remain humble.

I feel as though my family acknowledged these character traits in me early in my life. I feel it's part of the reason they relied on me in certain situations. I discerned that my mother and stepfather knew I would make something of myself; just by the way they talked to me at times. They'd hold mature conversations with me, often challenging me about things that were advanced for my age and grade level.

I developed a notion that they were counting on me to succeed, no matter how chaotic our lives might have been at the time. I've always appreciated overcoming challenges and obstacles, and each time I did, it gave me the confidence and strength I needed to get through the next challenge.

One thing I can say is, I admired my mother's and stepfather's belief in me. They saw ambition I didn't know I had. The look on my mother's face when she was proud of something I had achieved was priceless. It meant the world to me that she felt that way. In the midst of everything going on at home, if she couldn't believe in herself, *she could believe in me.*

I recall a time when my neighbor and I had planned to go swimming and have fun at Lake Calhoun. My mother gave me permission to go, and I was stoked. I looked forward all week to the arrival of that day. When it finally arrived, my neighbor changed her mind at the last minute. I was exasperated with her.

I felt down for a while, but then decided I wasn't going to let her control my happiness and destiny. I asked my mom if I could still go, and she said yes. I vividly recall the look on her face as I walked past her, down the stairs, and on my way. I was around 11 years old.

Judging from her smile, I could tell she was proud that I wasn't letting anyone or anything stop me from going to the lake. I walked three miles each way.

I had a great time all by myself, and I was happy I hadn't let anything stop me from going.

Initially, I'd been discouraged and considered not going because I was afraid to do it on my own. Going ahead by myself made it easier for me to be unafraid of taking chances on my own. It taught me to draw on my inner strength and muster up enough confidence to believe in myself that I could achieve anything I set my mind to.

I'd never gone to such a place alone. In fact, I didn't think it would be as much fun. I was glad I did it because, not only was it fun, I had also entered uncharted territory—meaning that it opened me up to an entirely new understanding of knowing my limits and how far I could go.

I was no longer afraid to experiment with things on my own or to go to new places. I felt more responsible and trusted myself from that day forward.

That day made me aware that I was in full control of my own destiny, and that no one could get in the way of it!

■ ■ ■

According to an article published by *Stay Teen* in March, 2015 (*https://www.dosomething.org/us/facts/11-facts-about-teen-pregnancy*), fewer than 2 percent of teen moms earn a college degree by age 30. Also, parenthood is the leading reason that teen girls drop out of school. More than 50 percent of teen mothers never graduate from high school.

When I became pregnant, I didn't know how I was going to raise a child, considering I was still one myself. I wasn't legally of age to work a job that would provide adequate financial support for just myself, let alone a kid, too. It all seemed impossible at first, even though I had the support of my son's father. I knew I had to become independent and financially secure immediately. The only way that would happen was for me to work as much as I could while I finished high school, then graduate from college and find a career job where I would earn a decent wage or salary.

I strategized to come up with a plan with short-term and long-term goals. My short-term goals consisted of immediate financial support that would pay for diapers, milk, food, clothes, medical expenses, childcare, fuel, and money to get by. This couldn't be the ordinary minimum wage job, so I had to be selective but aggressive in finding a job that offered benefits and an opportunity to earn higher wages. It also had to be economically feasible for me to get to and from the job each day, via bus or car.

My long-term goals were to choose a college major where I could get a job that paid a starting salary far above average. I knew it had to be in a competitive field where skills and experience were high in demand.

It wasn't easy executing this plan. I had to ask myself two questions: Do I want to live like I'm living right now for the rest of my life? Or, do I want to invest the time now to get educated and build a career that would afford me and my child a better quality of life with better opportunities?

I learned from experience that working regular minimum wage jobs wasn't providing an affordable living or improving our quality of life. I had to work multiple jobs just to earn a mediocre living. I knew the next several years would be an investment in my future.

I bit the bullet and focused my efforts for the next four to five years on college, while focusing less on the outside world. My social life and how I spent my spare time changed. I'd had to make necessary adjustments if I wanted to finish. With little time outside of studying and working, I spent time with my son.

After renting my first apartment and adjusting to more responsibility for several years, I dreamed of owning a home in a prestigious neighborhood located in North Minneapolis, off Victory Memorial Parkway. There weren't many black homeowners in this older neighborhood of beautiful, well-maintained homes, but I didn't let that stop me from dreaming and hoping I planned and set goals to meet the qualifications for buying a home there (saving for a down payment, working to get my credit up to par, and researching first-time homeowner programs).

As I worked toward meeting all the requirements, I'd frequently drive through the neighborhood, looking for my dream home.

The day finally came when I found it—the home of my dreams.

One Saturday morning, as I took my routine drive through the neighborhood, I saw what I thought was the most beautiful house in the area, and it had a "For Sale" sign in the yard. I was so excited and so busy looking at the house that I hit a car parked in front of it.

What a wreck I was, literally! I could barely hold in my excitement and joy. I contacted my agent, went through the process, and was approved for my first mortgage! This was one of the happiest, most fulfilling days of my life. At that moment, I felt my hard work had paid off. The sacrifices, sweat and tears had all been worth it. I was ecstatic to be a first-time homebuyer at the age of 25, and to give my son a place we could call our own.

But this was only the beginning. I continued to pursue my dreams, so that we could move onto greater and bigger things—furthering my education and building a lucrative career.

After earning my Associate's Degree in Applied Science, I immediately looked for opportunities within the company for which I was already working. I was fortunate to find a position that fit my degree. I applied, I interviewed, and I was offered the job.

Once acclimated to my new position, I learned more in the IT space, and knew I'd have to keep learning if I was to keep up with or stay ahead of the competition.

An Associate's Degree wouldn't get me there. So, I went back to school and majored in Computer Science/Information Technology. I hoped that this would give me broader experience and even better opportunities in IT. Some of the math classes (which had been one of my favorite subjects) were a lot tougher than I thought they'd be.

There were days when I didn't know how I was going to get through an assignment. There were nights when I was in tears and felt hopeless. I wanted to give up during these times when the semester's end seemed so far off.

Something inside me kept telling me I could do it and finish. I asked for one-on-one help from my instructors, tutors, and at group meetings. I successfully completed my challenging math classes and moved on to the next challenge.

Nine years into my career, I was ready for my next challenge, taking my career to a higher level. Opportunities with my employer at the time just weren't coming soon enough. I also wanted a completely new experience outside of Minnesota.

I longed to move to California, where the weather is beautiful most of the year. I was excited to find out what California had to offer. But I was terrified because of all the challenges in selling my home, finding the right job, raising my son on my own, and being such a long distance from his father (who, by the way, was still my support system), moving to a place without friends or family, and other challenges. I got discouraged for a moment, thinking it would be impossible and that I was out of my mind.

I decided one day to set my fears aside and take a chance on my dream. I put my house on the market and looked for jobs in California.

Several interviews later, I landed the right opportunity. I immediately began to look online for places to live and found the right place.

We settled into our new home, I acclimated to my new job, then I looked into furthering my education as part of an important career move. A few years later, I completed my MBA and was offered an opportunity that took my career to the next level, a new challenge with increased responsibilities, and options to learn different things.

I was so happy that I had taken a chance and hadn't given in to my fears. It wasn't easy, but I'm glad I charted the course. Turns out, it was one of the best things I could have done for my son and me. It not only taught me that we have to take risks and follow our dreams; it also showed my son that anything is possible if you give it your all and have faith in yourself.

When I became a mother at the age of 15, I was far from being financially secure enough to afford the necessities of raising a child. At first, I didn't know how I was going to provide for my son. I wasn't of legal age to work, and I wasn't sure what I wanted to be when I grew up.

During my pregnancy, I was often stressed about my short-term and long-term future. I knew I had to figure something out, and sitting around collecting welfare was not it. I worked lots of part-time hours when my son was born and while I finished high school. It was hard staying on top of my schoolwork and studies, attending to my son's needs, and going to work. It didn't seem like there were enough hours in the day for all of this, or enough strength to get through each day.

Once I finished high school, I could work full-time and go to college in the evenings. One job barely paid the bills, so I got a part-time job, while going to college full-time. This schedule meant I spent a lot of time away from my son, and the income was barely meeting our living expenses.

I did not want my son to know how much I was struggling to make ends meet, so I did my best to make our life look as normal as possible for him. And I did a good job hiding how I barely had enough money each day for his lunch and parking at work. I vowed that we would not live like this for long and that I would get us to a secure financial place where we didn't worry about these things. It became my mission to advance in my career and secure a job that challenged me and kept me abreast of constant technological changes.

As I took my career to the next level, my salary grew as well. I was earning a six-figure income while still in my twenties.

We still had a long way to go, but we had reached a point where we lived more comfortably and I didn't worry about things like lunch money, gas, and parking. I was in a place where I could not only afford necessities, but things I used to only dream of having.

When I first started driving, I could only afford to buy older model used cars. My income and credit didn't qualify me for newer, nicer cars. So, I had to settle for what they told me I could afford. I made it my goal and mission to change that by building my credit and increasing my income. I succeeded, and can now buy the car I want.

It felt degrading being denied and limited in what I could buy.

But it was the wakeup call I needed to improve my quality of life, including advancing in other areas, as well.

My graduation gift to me for completing my Master's Degree—after my son totaled my vehicle—was buying my dream car, a car I had wanted to own ever since I began driving. I was stoked! Not just because I had the keys to one of my dream cars, but because I had overcome the adversity of *not being qualified* to have something I wanted. I hadn't let rejection or disappointment keep me down. I knew, from the time I was first rejected or declined (metaphorically placed into a bucket), that I didn't want to feel this way, or experience this again.

Although I'd already bought several used cars before I could afford to purchase a vehicle of my choosing, it was the principle of not giving up on my dreams. For me, that made the initial rejection and disqualification worth it. Had I not experienced rejection, I probably wouldn't have pushed myself as hard to "never settle if you don't have to."

This one experience taught me the importance of being responsible and, conversely, what irresponsibility can reap. Rejection played a pivotal role in me wanting a better quality of life overall. The message I wanted to teach my son—and to reinforce within myself—is that it's rewarding when you work hard to achieve something, and hard work does pay off. The key is to not give up, and I didn't.

Life isn't about material things or status. It's about one's determination and willpower to make a difference. I started at the bottom, where my only option was to move up. Starting out, I didn't have a set path or destination for how far I would go, but I knew I had to know the difference between which path to take and which not to take.

My primary goal was to avoid the cycle of drug and alcohol addiction and abuse; I knew those things would definitely take me down the wrong path and prevent me from getting where I am today. I had to identify the things I needed to do to take the right path. There were certain lifestyles I knew to avoid. It would take discipline and a strict routine that I could stick to.

I had to find balance between achieving my goals and enjoying an interesting life. Although I had to make more sacrifices and work harder than I wanted to, I knew the rewards would be far greater in the end. Starting out, my future seemed bleak, but as I developed a routine and remained focused, my future became clearer. I may have stumbled through a few detours and run into obstacles along the way, but being able to minimize their impact and remain resilient helped me to stay the course. I did not lose sight of the end goal.

Key Takeaway from Chapter Twenty-Four
The light at the end of the tunnel.

More Takeaways...

- If I wanted better for myself, I couldn't just sit back and wait for it or depend on others to make things happen for me.

- Constant letdowns and disappointment from others inspired me to rely less on others and to not be afraid to take chances.

- Building independence and financial stability was my highest priority, aside from being a mother to my son.

- I created short-term and long-term goals: completing high school, graduating from college, and pursuing a career where I would earn a higher wage or salary.

- Completing each goal wasn't easy; however, the alternative encouraged me to stay the course.

- It took discipline, a routine, and attainable goals, while creating a healthy work-life balance.

- I stumbled and overcame several obstacles along the way, but I didn't lose sight of the end goal.

TWENTY-FIVE

Reflections

Having sober parents just wasn't in the cards for me. From the day I was born, I lived with parents who were chemically dependent or addicted to drugs and alcohol, who suffered or displayed physical abuse, and who had trouble staying on the path that would have kept them from hardship and pain. This experience has been both valuable and invaluable to me.

Looking back at all I've gone through, I truly believe that the experiences had a purpose, and that they have manifested in the person I am today and the person I am yet to become. Each experience, bump, scrape, and bruise correlates to my personality traits and characteristics.

I now understand that they were the tools and weapons that would equip me to take on a plethora of life's challenges. It makes more sense to me now why I endured certain situations, such as walking long distances alone in the dark at the age of 11 to get to and from school when I lived in the girls' shelter that was basically in no-man's land. This helped to prepare me for all that I would have to face on my own.

The circumstances I grew up in also taught me perseverance and determination. I was learning then not to settle for what was handed to me. I could have chosen to attend school in the shelter and take the easy way out. But, I refused to compromise my education; instead, I requested to go to my traditional school. It was a long shot, but having done it showed me that all things are possible if you believe. Being raised by alcohol and drug-addicted parents gave me firsthand experience of a lifestyle that I was 100 percent certain I did not want for myself or my loved ones. Going without the basic necessities taught me how to improvise and think outside the box.

Not having a constant, positive father figure in my life has taught me how important a father figure is when deciding to have children.

The lack of affection and attention from my mother taught me how important it is to hug and kiss my son every day, and let him know how much he means to me.

The many disappointments, the letdowns, and the abuse has thickened my skin and allowed me to be stern when needed.

The feeling of rejection and not fitting into "normal" society fueled my motivation to be more present and to help make a difference.

There was usually something positive for me to take from the negatives, and I decided to use my experiences as learning opportunities. What didn't kill me only made me stronger. My tenacity wouldn't allow me to give up or become defeated by my circumstances.

Triumph and victory prevailed at the end of every experience, which leads me to believe my Father in heaven was with me every step of the way! *He* never left or forsook me. *He* carried my load when it became too heavy for me to bear. *He* let me feel the wrath of my poor choices, but not to the point where I couldn't recover. *He* allowed me to cry and be sorrowful at thoughts of my past, but *He* didn't allow me to dwell in those moments for too long.

I believe *He* is expecting me to let go of all the hurt and pain, and look forward to a life-long journey of redemption. And I believe that it starts now *with this book.*

It won't happen overnight, and I don't have all the answers. I'm still figuring out this thing called life and where I fit in. I've made mistakes and poor choices along the way, but I do my best to learn from them and not repeat them. I realize that, as I grow wiser and more mature, I'm better able to make informed decisions and choices. I'm still a work in progress, and I'm grateful that I'm not where I used to be.

As I reflect on my life, I realize I may have done some things prematurely. Having sex and an unplanned pregnancy at such a young age changed my life in a way that forced me to become an adult overnight. It literally changed the way I had to live my life going forward, and do things that normally occur in adulthood.

I missed out on a lot of my childhood and youth because I had to make sacrifices and think like an adult, to care for my son. Although I don't regret having him, I would not recommend or condone other youth becoming parents at such a young age.

I advise younger generations to enjoy being adolescents and teenagers while they can.

I suggest that they enjoy high school and new beginnings as they transition to college.

The world has changed drastically since I became a mother, and certain things are much more challenging. With increasing global business and opportunities, securing career jobs may be more challenging than they were more than 15 years ago. I advise the younger generation to wait on parenthood, until they've created financial security and stability that will make them better-equipped to be parents.

I also suggest parenting with that special someone with whom you can spend the rest of your life.

Since my mother's passing, I've done a lot of soul-searching. My perspective, that she failed miserably at motherhood, has changed. For one thing, I'm taking into consideration how life must have been for her, especially growing up without her natural mother. Being separated from her mother when she was two weeks old must have left a void that no one could ever fill.

This thought was unfathomable for me, and it gave me a new

appreciation and empathy for my mother. She, too, was at a disadvantage when she brought us into this world. She didn't know what it was like to experience motherly love and affection. When I consider this, I feel she did a bang-up job, no pun intended, with the little example set by her big sister and stepmom.

As to having our mother only part of the time while we were growing up, she did the best she knew how, through trial, errors, oppression, and experiences, by teaching us to rely more on God than on her. I get it now, that God didn't put her on this earth or in our lives to be Mother of the Year, or Soccer Mom. I believe, instead, *He* wanted her to instill faith in us, and to build a solid connection between God and us, so that He could pick up where she fell short. If I must say so myself, she aced it!

After 30-plus years, I get how my mother did the best she knew how as a single parent. Although she fell short on numerous occasions, she died trying. Where I failed was in not considering that she was human and not perfect. I've been so caught up in my emotions and feelings that I didn't realize my expectations may have been unrealistic and flat-out unfair, especially considering the hand she was dealt starting out in life. I expected her to be a perfect mother, instead of the best mother she knew how to be. I had forgiven others who let me down, but I was unwavering with her.

Of all the people in this world, she should have been the one I was the most forgiving of. I should have been more compassionate about her early-life disadvantages, and I should have been more empathetic and less judgmental. Perhaps this new understanding would have made a difference in both our lives.

I'm grateful I finally reached a point where I could see things differently, but I'm extremely saddened it didn't happen before she left me. It's taken all my life to get to this realization, but I'm glad to have made this breakthrough.

Instead of focusing on what I don't have, I'll try to be more optimistic and look for the good. Some of my experiences have been invaluable lessons that made a positive difference in my life, because I witnessed, firsthand, the consequences and outcomes of certain actions. They taught me how to prevail when it seemed that things couldn't get worse. Also, they opened doors in my life that allowed for change.

When I was removed from our home, the experience allowed me to see how life was lived outside the conditions in which I lived. I met people who brought a different perspective and who gave me positive advice. The experiences gave my siblings and me counseling that helped us through tough times. Had we not been temporarily placed in homes, who knows what would have happened to us.

I believe in my heart some of these things happened to make my siblings' lives, my life, and our mother's life better. This thought brings me peace and consolation that, regardless of how dark our past was, there was always hope for a brighter future.

Key Takeaway from Chapter Twenty-Five

Life truly has a purpose.

More Takeaways...

- Every experience, scar, and pain manifested into the person I am today and have yet to become.

- Each experience, scar, and pain was a tool or weapon I needed to get through *life in its rawest form.*

- Despite the negativity, there was usually something positive for me to take from it.

- Triumph and victory won at the end of every experience, which leads me to believe my Father in heaven was with me every step of the way.

- Instead of focusing on what I didn't have, I tried to be optimistic and look for the good.

- I have control over my life, and *I* determine how I allow my past to affect my future.

- Regardless of how dark the past may be, there is always hope for a brighter future.

CONCLUSION

For many years, I became overwhelmed with sorrow when I reflected on events in my life, most of them pertaining to neglect and abuse from my mother; being deprived of the love and affection I felt I needed and never received; and longing but never receiving love and support from my father. Periodically, I would sit and think about them, or I would see or hear something that brought me back to those moments.

Many nights, I cried myself to sleep. Many days, I couldn't function during those moments of reflection. Eventually, I had to choose to either drown in sorrow and pain, or fight to overcome the pain by using those events as learning opportunities; opportunities that would make me a better person, mother, and sister. Early on, I knew I had to lead by example to make a difference in our lives. Someone had to change the vicious cycle, and that someone was *me*.

It was my duty to finish school and further my education, to show my family what a difference it can make in one's life.

It was my duty as a young mother and sister to show my loved ones what independence looked like by working as much as needed to provide for us, instead of waiting for someone to do it for me.

It was my duty to show them to never give up and to persevere to make your dreams happen.

It was also my job to show them that our lives didn't need alcohol or drugs, and to show them how I avoided affiliating with people who were into that lifestyle. I wasn't perfect, but I was determined to show my family a better way of life.

The most valuable lesson I learned in my life is that no one is exempt from being responsible and accountable for their choices, unless, of course, they are mentally and physically incapable.

For those people who have had a front row seat on how havoc and trouble can result from certain actions, I believe they should learn from others *what to do and what not to do.* I personally felt the pain and fear that substance abuse creates for a person and their loved ones. I vowed to never put my son through that, or anything close to it.

I experienced, firsthand, what life would be like, look like, and feel like without an education or career, and how it affects a person and their family: it limits and demoralizes them.

I never want to see my son starve or go without basic necessities, such as water, food, gas, electricity, and clean clothes. So, I knew *failure was not an option.*

I never wanted my son or my sister to experience any physical or sexual abuse, so I made sure I was an attentive mother and sister, and protected them as if my own life depended on it. I made sure to never put them or myself in situations where others could harm them. I was attentive to them, and showed them love and affection, so they didn't feel unloved or uncared for in any way. I made sure I didn't live a lifestyle that would compromise my being there for them, or put them at risk. I had to think responsibly and live my life accordingly, and I did that to the best of my ability.

It was extremely important for me to make sure that my son had a father who was in his life and showed him what fathers do for their children. I did not want him to experience being fatherless, as I had.

Having shielded my loved ones from the challenges I went through taught me how to be a better person to them. Pain and irony helped me learn, at an early age, the person I would and would not become. My challenges taught me to be the best I could be, and because of the outcome, the sacrifices were worth it.

If I wasn't before, I am now a firm believer that "Everything happens for a reason." All that I endured made me the person I am today. I'm appreciative that I could grow from the pain and mistakes of my past to provide a better future for myself and my loved ones.

Overall, life has taught me valuable lessons in the *rawest* form. Earlier, I never thought I could forgive my mother for the rocky upbringing she gave us, nor did I even consider that there might be a reason behind it. I never thought I could see myself walking in her shoes and seeing life from a broader perspective.

If I could change one thing, I would give my mother a chance to grow up with her biological mother. I can't help but wonder if things would have turned out differently had her mother been present in her life. I can't imagine what this void must have felt like for her. Perhaps her mother's love would have made a difference in the choices she made, and the type of mother she was to us.

Another lesson life has taught me is not to judge people based on their actions; there could be layers of stories indirectly correlating to their lives. I also learned that one addiction is no better or worse than another, and habits aren't always easy to overcome.

There were times in my life when I battled food addiction, and I gained an enormous amount of weight. Trying to overcome that addiction, I failed many times before I triumphed. It was then that I realized how difficult it must have been for my mom to overcome her substance abuse habits. I realized it's not as simple as "just stopping" because it's the right thing to do for the sake of others. It truly is a mental sickness and an ongoing battle.

I really believe my mom fought for us during her battle with drugs. I witnessed her never giving up, and trying to recover every time she relapsed. I saw the disappointment etched on her face when she failed. She was human, and now I get it. She wasn't perfect as a mother, and neither am I. She was a single mother who did her best to raise three kids, mostly on her own, and realizing that is now what matters most to me.

As I grew spiritually, thanks to my mother, I realized how the flesh in me wanted to hate my mother, but the spirit in me is now content, because I realize it was all a part of God's plan to make me into the person I am today. I had to endure challenges back then to prepare me for even bigger ones ahead. I get that, too.

What matters most are the principles, the morals, and values my mother taught us. Even if those moments were few and far between, they were meaningful and impactful. They planted the seeds we needed as we grew. My mother laid the foundation and left it up to us to build on it. She provided the tools and opportunities necessary to learn from her mistakes. I feel like she sacrificed her life so that we could have a better one. We learned that poverty magnifies chances for long-term hardship and misfortune. This helped us choose our path in life. Overall, I believe she did what she was put on this earth to do as a mother, and she did it to the best of her ability. And for that, I am grateful.

No matter where you come from, what's important is that you can choose to not let your past define who you are. No one can force you to become someone that you do not want to be. Life is what you make of it. You can choose to let past experiences or the things you lacked deter you from bettering yourself. Or, you can choose to be different, make the best of what you have and what you've overcome, and make a difference in your own life and potentially in others' lives.

In fact, if you're thinking this way, then you've already started. It's just a matter of putting your choices in motion to make your life your reality. I'm no longer ashamed of where I came from. In fact, I embrace it; I am wiser because of it. Wise enough to use those experiences as a way to make informed decisions and to keep an open mind.

If I can share my growth and experiences in hopes of inspiring just one person, then it's all been worthwhile.

LETTER TO MY MOMMY

A wise, spiritual friend suggested that I write you this letter. At first, I thought it was the dumbest idea I had ever heard. Then I realized it was brilliant.

When you were here, I wasn't metaphorically able to close many chapters in my book of life. In trying to complete them, I've always felt something was missing or didn't belong. Through an epiphany, I realize I've had what I was looking for all along, but it was suppressed by sorrow, pain, and fear.

It wasn't until you left me that I realized I had all the answers, words, and tools to complete the incomplete chapters. I was too wounded and afraid to tap into them. I was shrinking from my pain, at first, but now, through God, I see things clearly. Since you left, I've had no choice but to reflect and figure these things out on my own. I no longer had you to blame or use as an excuse for not getting what I needed.

I've forced myself to stop weeping, to feel blessed and thankful for everything you've done. Unfortunately, I'm not able to tell you that, now, I celebrate you as a mother and the best teacher I could ever have had. You taught me the *ultimate lessons of life*. Good and bad, the lessons you taught were the ones that resonated the most, and would substantially help me in all that I have yet to face in life.

When you left, I felt I'd never get the chance to tell you about the things I've held onto, and that I've been unsuccessful in overcoming. I was hoping I could tell you one day, and you would do your "mommy magic" to take the pain away, or help me reach a point where these things no longer affected me. When you died, I thought you'd no longer be able to hear me or make me feel better.

Now I realize you can still hear and feel me, and you've just taken a different seat in my life that I have to adjust to.

Mom, so much happened during the times we were abandoned due to your addictions. I've carried these burdens for a long time, and I don't want to carry them any longer. They weigh on me, and I literally have no more room for them to grow. I need to tell you these things, so that I can let them go and lighten my burden. Before I go into these things, first let me tell you how we're all doing.

Earl's doing okay. He's doing his best to be a big brother to Rene and me—while at the same time getting on my last nerve—and being a father to his daughters in ways our dads fell short. We've hit some bumps, but nothing that we won't overcome together.

Rene is well. She's working hard and doing great at being independent. Every time I look at her, I see you. She's so precious to me, still, but we're having a hard time with one another. I know we'll work it out, but I thought you should know. I wish you were here to fix things and put them into perspective, but I guess you'll just have to leave it to us to figure out, and I don't doubt that we will. Some things will just take time.

I'm still figuring things out and finding my way. There were times when I really could have used your touch, scent, and reassurance that I would get over the heartache and pain I experienced when I took a chance at love again. I think a lot of what I'm going through is magnified by the fact that I miss you, Mama. We all miss you. It's so hard not having you here with us. It hurts so badly, and I can't seem to make the pain go away. Eight years later and I still can't feel okay and at peace with having lost you. I need you so much.

I didn't get a chance to have you the way I wanted, and it was unfair. There were so many times and so many situations where I needed you to come get me. I looked to others to give me what I needed from you, only to end up hurt even worse.

Mommy, I have always loved you, but sometimes I had a tough way of showing it. Sometimes, I had to show you tough love, but those times hurt *me* even more. You are the one who taught me how to be so tough and stern when need be. I was tired of getting hurt by you. You were the one person on this earth who could protect me and make me feel whole, and you didn't always do that. You teased me with short periods of sobriety, then you violently snatched those moments away when you got high or drunk. I felt like a lot of the atrocities that happened to us were because of your failures. I felt like we wouldn't have been put in those situations if you had just put us first.

I was selfish and didn't want to think about the things that happened to you throughout your life that caused you to do the things you did. I was too naïve to understand that you, too, suffered pain and disappointment that went unresolved. However, I do get it now, and I just want to tell you how sorry I am for blaming you.

Until now, I didn't know how to be impartial. I get it now and I just want you to know that I love and appreciate all that you have done for me. I no longer blame you for these things, and I want to apologize for holding you responsible all of these years.

I just want to say that I love and miss you.

ABOUT THE AUTHOR

Qiana Hicks grew up in an environment with few resources and opportunities. Most would not expect her to succeed or escape as a result of her environment. The most widely-accepted statistics, in fact, report that, under such circumstances, she would fail, while very few statistics dared to report the opposite. Qiana can be counted among the few that defied those statistics.

Her purpose in writing about her struggle to break the mold isn't to brag or boast, but to simply prove to the doubters and naysayers that anything is possible, whether we're born into fortunate or unfortunate circumstances. Ultimately, we individuals control our destiny—and, according to Ms. Hicks, that reality can never be minimized.

The point of Qiana's story is to inspire others to beat the odds and succeed—regardless of the obstacles life throws at them. Never give up and never stop dreaming. Have faith that, with perseverance, you'll have what it takes to overcome the impossible, all while remaining humble and modest. Then help others do the same, in return and in gratitude for your victory and blessings.

ALSO WRITTEN BY AUTHOR QIANA HICKS

Companion Workbook

I wrote this *Companion Workbook* to *Life In Its Rawest Form* to help empower *you*—no matter what your background—to overcome challenges from your past. *Challenges that may be holding you back from achieving your best possible life.*

Growing up, I dreamed of a better future, but I had no one in my life who could just hand it to me. So, *it was up to me.* I figured out how to plan for my future by setting goals for myself. And, one day at a time, I accomplished each goal.

How did I turn my dreams into plans, goals, and a better future? My "formula," and how it can help *you*, is all laid out and waiting for you in the *Companion Workbook*.

This workbook will be your "toolkit" to guide you in setting attainable goals and creating plans and strategies that give you power over your past.

I'm putting my tools into *your* hands.

Use them, as instructed throughout the *Companion Workbook*, and watch how you'll be making better decisions that will lead to a brighter future. Whether you're a child, a youth, or an adult, you'll learn how to proactively seek opportunities that will make your life better and improve your circumstances.

Others who will benefit from the *Companion Workbook*...

Family Services agencies, educators, foster homes, group home staff and administrators, mentors, youth advocates, community outreach programs, disadvantaged youth workers, at-risk youth, teen parents, drug-and alcohol-addicted parents, family and friends of those battling drug and/or alcohol addiction.

The Companion Workbook will also help you help others to break away from destructive and disruptive influences that practically guarantee that the cycle repeats for yet another generation. It will help family and friends of drug- or alcohol-addicted loved ones know how to help them.

Companion Workbook Chapters:
Seven chapters that will change your life (for the better)

Each chapter includes interactive exercises and information to inspire you, uplift you, and improve your situation and circumstances.

Chapter 1. Families Battling Addiction

Chapter 1 discusses common issues and concerns that exist within families where one or both parents battle drug or alcohol addiction.

Exercises include defining how their addiction(s) affect you. Express your thoughts and feelings, then share them with your parent(s). Make them aware of how *their* behavior affects *your* behavior. Share your hopes that they will change for the better.

Chapter 2. Families In Transition

Chapter 2 focuses on making you aware of how transition will affect you and your family. We identify how Family Services professionals can help minimize the impact of the process. We also explore how to effectively cope with the changes you'll experience.

In my book, *Life In Its Rawest Form*, I talk about my experiences and how they impacted my life. I describe my emotional rollercoaster, my challenges with living in temporary placement facilities, and the types of help I wished I'd had to manage my transition positively.

Chapter 3. Teenage Pregnancy

Chapter 3 discusses opportunities for getting the help and support I wasn't fortunate enough to have, to prevent or lessen chances of becoming an adolescent parent. We explore prevention methods, and, if you're already an adolescent parent, we provide options that offer a brighter future. Some of the topics we'll cover are:

- Preventive Measures:
  - > Ways to prevent teenage pregnancy
  - > Love and relationships without sex
  - > Using time constructively

- Acknowledgment:
  - > Acknowledge the reason(s) you became a parent
  - > Understand the consequences
  - > Know the impact to you and others

- Defeating the Odds:
  - > A plan for a brighter future
  - > Better decision making
  - > Overcoming obstacles early on
  - > Not letting your current situation define your future

- Breaking the Cycle:
  - > Dare to be different
  - > Learn from your past
  - > Be an example to others
  - > Do not let your surroundings influence you

Chapter 4. Setting Goals And Executing Them

The main goal of Chapter 4 is to define goals—short- and long-term—and develop a plan for executing them.

What goes into achieving goals? Hard work and sacrifices. We also discuss that aspect.

Chapter 5. Choosing The Right Role Model For You

It's vitally important to your future to choose the right role model. Chapter 5 discusses good role models and not-so-good role models. You'll learn how to distinguish between the two, and how to steer clear of the not-so-good ones. You'll identify which qualities and characteristics to look for when deciding on the best role model for you.

Chapter 6. Leaving The Past In The Past

Chapter 6 explores methods for *effectively* acknowledging and dealing with our past. We identify ways to live with our past without letting it create unhealthy behavior or post-traumatic stress.

Chapter 7. Managing Your Emotions Effectively

Life doesn't always happen the way we want it to happen. At times, we're faced with situations that are out of our control and that challenge us to find solutions. Chapter 7 helps you to become aware of your emotions, identify with them, and create opportunities to manage them effectively. You'll improve your life and the situation at hand.

The best part of owning the *Companion Workbook* to *Life In Its Rawest Form* is it can be used more than once. Use it regularly. Use it as a reference guide to track your progress. Share it with others, so they can learn how they can help you and others.

Visit my website at www.qianahicks.com

Made in the USA
Columbia, SC
03 August 2021